THE REFORMATION IN 100 FACTS

KATHLEEN CHATER

First published 2016

Amberley Publishing
The Hill, Stroud
Gloucestershire, GL5 4EP

www.amberley-books.com

British Library Cataloguing in Publication Data.
A catalogue record for this book is available from the British Library.

ISBN 978 1 4456 5134 7 (paperback)
ISBN 978 1 4456 5135 4 (ebook)

Typeset in 11pt on 13.5pt Sabon.
Typesetting and Origination by Amberley Publishing.
Printed in the UK.

The Facts

Introduction

The Reformation is one of the most significant events in history. We could perhaps go as far as to say *the* most significant event that has shaped our modern world, and its effects still reverberate today. Even those who profess no religion are shaped by the cultures created by the believers of the past. Although the names remain the same, our sixteenth and seventeenth-century ancestors would not recognise the churches, both Protestant and Roman Catholic, that have evolved from the early reform movements. To try to encapsulate such complex and continuing effects and developments in 100 facts is impossible. I have concentrated on the British Isles, but I hope this book will encourage people to learn more.

1. POLITICS TRUMPS RELIGION

Both politics and religion aim to direct how people live their lives so inevitably that they become enmeshed. Whatever faith the ruling classes profess, ultimately they will act in their own best political interests. During the Reformation this meant finding some way to apply a religious spin to justify their actions. Conveniently the Bible, like all sacred texts, contains enough internal contradictions to make this possible. Religious belief was sacrificed to temporal power with long-term consequences when the monarchs of England (Henry VIII), France (Louis XIV) and Spain (Philip II) took administrative control over the Church in their respective countries, with the monarch having the final say in appointments to senior Church positions, whether Protestant or Catholic. The cascade effect ensured that those lower down would also toe the party line.

Shorter-term examples of opportunism can be found in the wars triggered by religion which developed into political conflict: between 1560 and 1715 there were only thirty years of peace across Europe. The Thirty Years War was set off when those not keen on the Catholic Holy Roman Empire's dominance over their realms adopted Protestantism instead. Even so, Catholic France supported some of the German states involved and also assisted the Protestant Netherlands in their struggle for independence from Catholic Spain. Even the Pope later joined in, backing Protestant England against the French support of James II's attempts to regain his throne, and England tried to back the winning side, whatever its religion.

2. THE CATHARS WERE THE FIRST REFORMERS

Around AD 940 a religious sect was first noticed in the Balkans, led by a Bulgarian named Bogomil. No one knows where his beliefs originated. His followers were Christian but had some decidedly unorthodox beliefs, a few of which they shared with (or maybe adopted from) religions in the Middle East. The main difference between them and the Catholic Church of the day was their conviction that the world was governed by two equal principles: good and evil. Good was the God of the New Testament and Evil was the God of the Old, which they identified as the Devil. This was against the Catholic Church's teachings that there was one God who created everything.

There were a number of other groups holding this dualist view. Some were known as Cathars (the pure ones) this has become applied to the entirety of this particular sect. Not all their beliefs and teachings are known – they had to keep their heads down as they were soon branded heretics. What is known is that followers were divided into two groups: the Perfects, those who were more advanced on the road to ultimate salvation; and the Believers, the average man or woman in the medieval street. Catharism taught that human souls were angels trapped in the body, which was evil, and they were doomed to reincarnation until, through rigid discipline and ascetic practices, they were freed by the *consolamentum* (consolation), a deathbed ceremony like the last rites administered by the Catholic Church.

Like the Catholics, they held that celibacy was a holier estate than marriage, but they gave women greater religious power; women could become Perfects, who alone could administer the *consalamentum*. No doubt helped by this liberal attitude to females, by the 1140s the growth of followers in Italy and France was beginning to seriously alarm the papacy. Cathars were respected by their neighbours, and even some local bishops admired their moral behaviour, so different from so many Catholics. A spate of missionaries failed to convince them to recant. Finally, in 1208, soldiers were brought in and the Albigensian Crusade was launched against the stronghold of Catharism in the south of France. Over the next twenty years a series of massacres wiped out whole communities here. Those who fled were hunted down by the Inquisition and the last known French Perfect was executed in 1321. The Cathars lasted longer in Italy. Here they were mainly absorbed back into the Catholic Church through missionary activity, although there were some massacres. Those who refused to recant fled to Piedmont, the mountainous refuge of other persecuted heretics.

Two centuries before Martin Luther, Catharism was the greatest threat to the Roman Catholic Church. Although they shared some of the later reformers' beliefs, such as denial that in the Eucharist the bread and wine became the actual body and blood of Christ, Cathars did not profess the five tenets of mainstream Protestantism. They protested against what they saw as the corruption of the Catholic Church, which they identified with the Devil, but they were not Protestants.

3. MARTIN LUTHER WAS THE FIRST TO CHALLENGE THE ROMAN CATHOLIC CHURCH DIRECTLY

Before the Reformation, the most seismic upheaval came in 1204 when the Catholic Church finally split off from the original Orthodox Church following centuries of spats over major and minor points of theology. It quickly established control over religion in Western Europe and easily saw off Cathars, Hussites and Waldensians, largely by massacring them. Others, like the Franciscans, whose emphasis on poverty was embarrassing, were absorbed. Individuals, like Galileo, could be picked off individually and silenced. The whole history of Christianity has been one of challenges and fallings out among the faithful.

Martin Luther was not the first to criticise the power of the Pope. One of the most influential of the early aspiring reformers was the English scholar and theologian John Wycliffe, who was distinctly underwhelmed by the papacy. His followers acquired the nickname of Lollards, probably meaning mutterers, but whatever its etymology the term was derogatory, applied to those who had no university education. Those who had an academic background were called Wycliffites, which sounds a lot more respectable. It wasn't just snobbery that caused the Lollards to be condemned as heretics. In 1365 they posted a petition on the door of Westminster Hall, the administrative centre of the government. It called for a return to the Bible, criticised the focus on wealth and greed in the Church, questioned the doctrine of transubstantiation in the Eucharist, rejected the cult of relics, claimed praying for the dead was a distraction from caring for the living and, probably the most dangerous of their demands, called for a lay priesthood, saying the Church did not have any authority to create priests. Wycliffe, by now a Doctor of Divinity, was thrown out of Oxford University in 1381, and shortly afterwards he and his associates completed and published a translation of the Vulgate Bible from Latin into English, the third complete vernacular Bible in Europe (a French translation was published in the late thirteenth century and a Czech one appeared in 1360). Although he frequently had to explain himself to the Bishop of London, the Archbishop of Canterbury or other religious authorities, the English were going through one of their anti-foreigner phases and refused to have him excommunicated or punished. Wycliffe managed to die a natural death while celebrating Mass in 1384. Thirty-one years later, he was declared a heretic, his writings banned and his body dug up and burned.

John Wycliffe, Jan Hus and Peter Waldo shared common views on the faults of the Church of their day that foreshadowed Martin Luther's tenets. Although he supposedly nailed up his controversial document in a prominent place, as the Lollards did, there is no evidence Luther was influenced by them. It was possible to silence these early critics and destroy evidence of their teachings. Luther was just the latest in the line of members of the awkward squad. Because of the particular political, social and technical factors of his age, he became the first to *successfully* challenge the Catholic Church's virtual monopoly of faith in Europe.

4. WILDCARDS 1: WALDENSIANS

The Cathars were not the only French sect to threaten Catholicism. Pierre Vaudès or de Vaux (known now as Peter Waldo) was a merchant living in Lyons, France, in the twelfth century. Around 1160 he decided to get rid of his property and follow the Biblical injunction that no one can obey God and Mammon. His views attracted a number of followers, known as the Poor Men of Lyon or the Poor of God. This might have led to the founding of an Order within the Catholic Church, as Francis of Assisi would later do. However, Waldo also rejected some of the Catholic Church's teachings, such as the existence of Purgatory, and criticised the lifestyle of the Pope of the day, calling him the anti-Christ and the Church the harlot of the Book of the Revelation of St John, whose appearances are said to prefigure the end of the world, as Martin Luther would do more than three centuries later. Unsurprisingly, this did not go down well with the Pope and Waldo was summoned to Rome in 1179 to explain himself. His beliefs were declared heretical in 1184 and he and his followers were driven away from Lyons.

The predicted end of the world did not manifest itself so the believers needed somewhere to live. They initially took refuge in the Dauphiné in south-east France and in neighbouring Piedmont, today in Italy, but then both ruled by the Duke of Savoy. In 1215 they were formally declared heretical and suffered great persecution, but even the order to exterminate them issued by Pope Innocent VII in 1487 did not deter them. Under the guise of peddlers, they spread their teachings, some of which predated the Protestant beliefs by many centuries, which undoubtedly paved the way for reform. As well as denying the existence of Purgatory, they did not regard relics or water that had been officially blessed as holy.

When Protestantism began to establish itself in Europe, the leaders of the day decided they and their followers should join local Protestant congregations as their beliefs were entirely compatible. Persecutions and massacres followed. One of the worst was in 1545 in Mérindol in Provence when several villages were destroyed and possibly thousands died. With the Edict of Nantes in 1598 they were granted some level of toleration in France, but elsewhere persecution continued. In 1655 the Duke of Savoy staged a massacre to wipe them out of his territory. Most of the survivors scattered to other places – like Germany, the Netherlands and the ultimate refuge for those fleeing religious persecution, North America – but a Waldensian Evangelical church based in Piedmont still survives today in Italy. There are also Waldensian Presbyterian churches in the USA, and communities in Germany. Uruguay even has a tiny outpost, called Colonia Valdense, founded near Montevideo in 1856 by a group of Piedmontese economic migrants, some of whose descendants still live there. The Waldensians remain one of the most enduring 'heretical' sects.

5. A Fourteenth-Century Heretic Has Inspired Resistance for 600 Years

The national hero of today's Czech Republic is Jan Hus, born in Bohemia in 1369. He studied at Prague University, where he later taught theology. Although he was a priest, he was not unusual in believing the Catholic Church of his day needed reform, but he went further, coming to espouse many of the later tenets of Protestantism, such as conducting services in native languages, putting more emphasis on Biblical teaching and banning the sale of indulgences. He was influenced by John Wycliffe and, like him, lived before the invention of printing, so did not have the technological means to spread his words quickly and widely. However, he convinced many people to agree with him and his followers were known as Hussites.

In 1412 news of his alarming teachings reached the Church's ever-sensitive ears and he was excommunicated for insubordination and failing to respect the authority of the Church. He was undeterred and a few years later the Holy Roman Emperor of the day, Sigismund, promised him safe passage to attend a meeting to present his beliefs. Sigismund ratted on his agreement and Hus was arrested. On his refusal to recant, he was tried for heresy and burned at the stake on 6 July 1415. This example of imperial duplicity – to be repeated when Martin Luther was in similar circumstances a century or so later – set off the Hussite Wars in 1419.

It wasn't just the emperor's treachery that foreshadowed future Protestantism. The Hussites split into two factions, broadly analogous to the Lutheran–Calvinist divide. The Catholics called them all heretics and the wars lasted until 1436. They ended when the more moderate Hussites returned to the Catholic Church, although they did wring some concessions from the Pope. This reunification didn't last long and a separate Church that did not recognise the Pope's authority was set up in Bohemia in 1457. No one wanted to set off another war and it was left to its own devices, evolving into a Church with fundamentally Protestant beliefs. The name chosen, the United Brotherhood, gives an indication of its political face, and it became a kind of party of opposition to the king. It did not, however, embrace the Reformation when it arrived. Determined to march to its own beat, it refused to become one of the Reformed churches, remaining Hussite.

Jan Hus remained a symbol of defiance of oppressive regimes for centuries, first against the Catholic Church, then against the Habsburg Empire, and more recently against communism. The day of his martyrdom, 6 July, is still celebrated as a national holiday in the Czech Republic. To commemorate the 500th anniversary of his death, a huge monument to him was erected in Prague's Old Town Square in 1915 using money made entirely from public donations. Sitting at Hus's feet was said to show opposition to communist rule. Now, the monument has been renovated for the 600th anniversary.

6. Without the Renaissance, the Reformation Would Not Have Happened

The term Renaissance (which means rebirth) was not coined until the nineteenth century. What the people who pioneered the movement called it was *studia humanitatis*, the study of human nature, known as humanism. This must not be confused with the modern use of the word for those who believe humans must take responsibility for solving problems, not wait for divine or supernatural intervention. The humanists of their day were Catholics.

It began around 1330 in Italy when the poet Petrach (1304–74) began to investigate little-known or forgotten ancient Roman writers. He was interested in how to apply philosophy to create a civilised society and his work led to a revival of interest in classical studies, initially Latin, but then Greek and even Hebrew. Those who developed the idea realised, less nobly, that studying the new disciplines (grammar, rhetoric, history, poetry, moral philosophy) would enable people to argue a case persuasively, to gain and use power and to pursue their ambitions more successfully.

It was the beginning of the idea of men as individuals, rather than a cog in a family, a race, a religion. Women remained regarded as fit only for household tasks while their menfolk got on with having Great Thoughts and running the world. Although a number of Great Thinkers fell foul of the religious enforcers because of the dangerous ideas they imbibed from pagan philosophers, some popes were humanist and most Renaissance writers were Roman Catholic. They might have needed to do a bit of linguistic juggling to accommodate some of the ancients' ideas about life and society into Christian beliefs, but they did not reject their Church's teachings.

There's always an awkward squad and some men found that their studies of Biblical texts began to raise doubts. Among the leaders of the early Reformation were humanists, but to make a direct link between the Renaissance and the Reformation is too simplistic. Although it is true that the Renaissance paved the way for the Reformation, not least in its emphasis on individuality, it was not the only factor. The Renaissance came at a time when increasing trade and travel outside of Europe was widening horizons. The narrow world of the medieval Church was opened up, especially through links with the Islamic Ottoman Empire, where to their astonishment Christians found learned and cultivated Muslims, not the barbarians of propaganda. The development of printing allowed ideas to be disseminated and argued as two people could use the same text as a basis for discussion. These two factors were also significant in the movement for reform.

In addition, the political situation of the sixteenth century and the manifest corruption of the Catholic Church of the time make it extremely likely that there would have been some kind of confrontation between those who wanted change and those who were happy with the status quo. A reformation would have happened without the Renaissance but whether it would have resulted in splitting Western Christianity into two camps remains a matter for debate.

7. The Term 'Holy Roman Empire' Is a Breach of the Trade Descriptions Act

For over a thousand years the Holy Roman Empire controlled a large swathe of central Europe from the North Sea to the Mediterranean. The name, not used until medieval times, showed that it marketed itself as a continuation of the old Roman Empire. In theory the emperor was elected, like the Roman head honchos, but in practice it became a family affair and the electors were made very aware who they should vote for. It was made up of a multi-ethnic patchwork of territories ranging in size from kingdoms, through principalities, dukedoms and counties, all the way down to individual towns. The emperors learned not to enquire too closely into what was actually happening at ground level as long as their subjects paid their taxes, and many states were more or less autonomous. This was not dissimilar to the original Roman Empire, but this 'Holy Empire' never got as far as Britain or North Africa, and didn't even manage to engulf France, which was its fiercest enemy for most of its existence.

'Holy' referred to the empire's Catholic ethos. The Pope of the day had crowned Charlemagne emperor in AD 800 and those who followed him felt they were the apple of the papal eye and had a special relationship. However, any Pope who stepped out of line would have been swiftly shown the error of crossing the emperor. This gave them an alarming degree of power. About the time the Reformation began, the Habsburg family controlled the empire and had acquired the throne of a newly unified Spain. The title 'The Most Catholic King' was awarded to the rulers of Spain. Emperor Charles V actually lived in Burgundy, then a flourishing separate kingdom covering considerably more than today's French province. With his brother Ferdinand installed in the empire's headquarters in Vienna and his son Philip in Madrid, the empire arguably became the most powerful political entity across Europe during the period of the Reformation, since it also ruled much of Italy, including the Papal States.

Though the Spanish Inquisition managed to suppress reform, elsewhere across the empire Protestantism flourished. The powerful German states in particular took to Protestantism, in many cases for political as well as, or even instead of, spiritual reasons. In 1555 Pope Paul IV, alarmed by the Habsburgs' vice-like grip, took the side of France in a dispute, whereupon Emperor Charles V realised his hopes of a world Christian empire led by him in the image of the original Roman one had been scuppered. For some time he had been transferring power over various territories to his son, and the next year he abdicated from the empire itself in favour of his brother.

'Empire' is probably the only completely accurate word in the title. For centuries it did rule an extensive domain across Europe and, by proxy, the Spanish colonies in the Americas. It was another emperor, Napoléon, who managed to bring about its ultimate downfall in 1806.

8. SWITZERLAND BELIEVES WAR IS NOT SENSIBLE

Switzerland has always tried to keep aloof from conflicts in other parts of Europe. This does not mean unilateral peace-and-love disarmament, as the Holy Roman Empire discovered in 1499. Imperial soldiers were sent to teach this rebellious possession a lesson after a territorial conflict erupted into the Swabian War. They soon discovered the Swiss were doughty fighters. From then on, Switzerland went its own sweet way without any further interference from its claimed rulers. Such was their reputation as loyal fighters that Swiss guards were hired by Pope Julius II in 1506. He needed his own private army and the Swiss were not controlled by any of the major powers in Europe at that time. They continue to serve in the Vatican today.

By the time of the Reformation the Swiss confederacy's original eight self-governing cantons had increased to thirteen. Huldrich Zwingli (1484–1531) was the major reformer here. Born in the canton of St Gallen, he was ordained as a Catholic priest but was strongly influenced by humanism, and developed his own ideas about reforming the Catholic Church independent of Luther, although they shared some similarities, such as the primacy of scripture. It is still disputed how much influence Luther had on Zwingli or vice versa. Zwingli persuaded the authorities and the people of Zurich to adopt reforms in the 1520s and his ideas spread to other cantons, most notably Geneva, where Calvin's more radical ideas took root. Though politically neutral, Switzerland could not remain uncommitted about the theological disputes that raged elsewhere. Seven cantons remained Roman Catholic.

As elsewhere in Europe, this conflict led to civil war: the two wars of Kappel in 1529 and 1531. However, wars waste people, time and effort and make the place dirty and untidy – all anathema to the practical and neat Swiss. The first war finished without a battle being fought, though one Catholic priest was executed and a Protestant pastor was burned at the stake. In the second war there was a single battle and a further skirmish, both of which the Protestants lost. This battle and its aftermath so horrified both sides that they negotiated a peace. This included the entirely enlightened agreement that in some territories the two factions would coexist, with both faiths even sharing the same buildings for worship – frugality being another Swiss characteristic. Though this led to later confrontations, including short-lived conflicts in 1656 and 1712, the peace generally held, allowing the industrious citizens of all cantons to get on with what they did best, from banking to making cuckoo clocks.

Peace at home did not stop Swiss mercenaries from taking important parts in the French Wars of Religion and the Thirty Years War in the German States. They had, over the years, honed their skills fighting armies who wanted to subjugate them. The end of the Thirty Years War in 1648 brought formal ratification of Swiss independence from the Holy Roman Empire and also formally established its neutrality.

9. THE ROMAN CATHOLIC CHURCH NEEDED REFORMATION

By the sixteenth century the Catholic Church was seriously corrupt and the rot started at the top. The job at the apex, the Pope, had been filled by a succession of worldly men, mainly from the powerful families of the Italian states, who shamelessly promoted their relatives' interests. Though supposedly celibate, the popes' beneficiaries often included their own children. Theoretically the Pope was chosen by the inspiration of the Holy Spirit, but between 1455 and 1978 only Italians held this post and it's statistically unlikely that the Holy Spirit could not find someone better from another region. In practice it was mainly the Spanish monarch who selected the Pope, with the French and the Austrian rulers having a veto which did not end until 1904. Someone elderly was also preferred so he wouldn't have too much time to get a grip on the job.

Although there were many good and holy people, the Pope's example was followed by the cardinals and other churchmen they appointed, along with the parish priests who ministered to the local congregations. The degree of laxity was undoubtedly exaggerated by reformers, but even Catholics found examples of permissive morals at all levels of the Church. Some orders of monks and friars did educate children and care for the poor and infirm, but they were in the minority. Closed monasteries and nunneries had become a place where a spare relative with no vocation could be lodged, especially if this could boost a local family's power. By accumulating relics – many of them faked – which people paid to see, they maximised their incomes but drained the economy of investment.

They supported an increasing number of people who contributed nothing to society and frequently had no vocation.

It was not just in worldly matters that the Catholic Church was remiss. In order to maximise income, Pope Sixtus IV (1471–84) invented 'indulgences', spiritual get-out-of-jail-free cards. Whatever sins had been committed, the payment of a fee supposedly assured an easy ride in the afterlife for an individual or his family. Paying for requiem masses and other ceremonies gave the rich a spiritual advantage over the poor. For the reformers, money was the main root of the Catholic Church's evils, but many other teachings and practices had no basis in Scripture. The Church taught that ordinary people could only deal with God via a priest or a saint, which reformers disputed. They also challenged the Church's claim to be able to remit sins or lessen a soul's time in Purgatory.

Earlier objectors, like Jan Hus in Moravia and John Wycliffe in England, had been silenced, but by the early sixteenth century reformers in a number of places all over Europe had reached a critical mass. Many people were aware of the problems, but too many people benefited from them for any headway to be made. Not even Catholics would now dispute the necessity for reform, but must regret that it did not come early enough to prevent a split.

10. A Thunderstorm Changed the Course of European History

The father of Martin Luther (1483–1546) ran a copper mine. No doubt his job convinced him that the law was a better career for a bright lad, who would be warm, dry, indoors and well paid. After his first university degree concentrating on theology and philosophy, in 1505 Martin was enrolled in law school, but very soon dropped out. It was partly that he did not like the law, but the catalyst for his momentous change of direction was a storm while he was riding back to university after a visit home. A lightning bolt narrowly missed him and, in fear of death and judgement, he called on St Anne for help and vowed to become a monk if his life was spared. He told his disappointed father he could not break his oath and entered an Augustinian friary.

Although it was a closed order Luther's talents were recognised, and a few years later, after ordination as a priest in 1507, his superior at the friary, now Dean of the University of Wittenberg, gave him a teaching post there. In 1512 Luther became a Doctor of Theology. Preparing lectures for students made him study in depth and begin to question the religious doctrines he later challenged. Without the thunderstorm, Luther might instead have spent his life as just another bourgeois German lawyer, musing on legal loopholes and how much he could charge his clients. If the lightning bolt had struck him, however, the name of Martin Luther would not even be a footnote in a local history book.

11. Martin Luther Nailed Ninety-Five Theses to the Church Door in Wittenberg

It's one of the best-known historical anecdotes how, on 31 October 1517, to the consternation of his fellow townsfolk, Martin Luther nailed ninety-five complaints about the Roman Catholic Church to the door of Wittenberg church. It's an iconic moment in religious history and has been reproduced in woodcuts, paintings, engravings, children's picture books and even stained glass. It has been shown in films and television programmes, but is it the whole story?

Most reproductions in whatever medium represent the event as a complete surprise, but it did not come out of the blue to Luther's superiors and colleagues. In 1510 he had spent a year in Rome, representing the German Augustinian monasteries, and was not impressed by the corruption he saw there. After gaining his doctorate in theology in 1512 Luther began to teach, and giving and preparing lectures on the Bible made him question the validity of many Catholic doctrines. Those around him must have been aware of his growing concerns, academia being a place built on questions and arguments.

Matters came to a head in 1516 when a papal commissioner toured Germany. He was selling indulgences to raise money to rebuild St Peter's in Rome, using the slogan, 'As soon as the coin in the coffer rings, the soul from Purgatory (or 'into heaven') springs.' Luther objected to this commercialisation of the road to eternal life. He spent time marshalling his ninety-five theses – carefully argued proposals for discussion – and on 31 October 1517 wrote to his archbishop objecting to the sale of indulgences. Luther probably did not know that the archbishop had paid to get his job and needed income from the indulgences to repay his debts. He included a copy of his 'Disputation on the Power and Efficacy of Indulgences'. Some scholars question whether a copy of the document was also actually nailed to the door on the same day he sent the letter. The story does not appear until after his death and Luther might not even have been in Wittenberg then. Either way, attaching a document to the church door was less confrontational than it might appear. Although this seems to be a challenge to the Church, it was at the time the usual place to pin up academic subjects for discussion and public notices because everyone was presumed to pass there.

Most of the features of the well-known story that people generally believe are factually inaccurate: the ninety-five theses were not complaints about the general state of the Church, they were an academic examination of the doctrine of indulgences, although they did incorporate criticisms of other teachings. Not many people could have been astonished: Luther's fellow academics must have known about his concerns and, as the theses were written in Latin, very few townspeople would have been able to understand them, let alone be outraged by their academic content. Whether or not Luther physically nailed the document to the door, he metaphorically drove a wedge that split the Catholic Church – that part at least is accurate.

12. Protestants Have to Believe Only Five Things

The reformers formulated five principles on which they believed the Christian Church should be based and they remain a quick way of assessing whether a sect is or is not Protestant.

1. *Sola scriptura* (by scripture alone). Only the Bible should inform beliefs and practices.
2. *Sole fide* (by faith alone). In Roman Catholicism salvation can be achieved by works, like saying the rosary or burning candles to strengthen prayers. For reformers, justification is by faith alone.
3. *Sole gratia* (by grace alone). Roman Catholicism teaches that the bread and wine are miraculously turned into the body and blood of Christ at the moment of communion (the doctrine of transubstantiation). Reformers believe that grace is God's unmerited gift and communion is a commemoration of the historic event of Christ's sacrifice.
4. *Sole Christus* (by Christ alone). In Roman Catholicism lay people cannot communicate directly with God, there has to be an intermediary, whether it is a priest or a saint, who approaches God on behalf of the supplicant. The reformers say that belief in Christ is enough and that the faithful can communicate directly with God through prayer.
5. *Soli Deo Gloria* (glory to God alone). All the saints, sacred relics, holy wells and the like endorsed by Roman Catholicism have no spiritual value. More fundamental reformers feel that images distract the faithful and might themselves become objects of veneration. This led to iconoclasm, the destruction of religious images in churches.

13. THE END OF THE WORLD IS NIGH

The Book of the Revelation of St John describes in highly symbolic and mystical terms the second coming of Christ and the end of the world. Early Christians believed it was imminent and for the best part of 2,000 years this has been a recurring claim. The appearance of Halley's Comet has sometimes been seen as a warning. In 1066 it was said to signal Armageddon, the final battle between good and evil. The Battle of Hastings, though important for English history, proved an anticlimax. The Crusades were launched to retake Jerusalem from the muslims, then seen as the Antichrist, the embodiment of evil who will appear just before Christ's second coming, prefiguring the end of the world.

The Protestant belief in the Bible as the literal truth has meant that the end of the world has been a recurring theme for Protestant sects since the Reformation. Martin Luther identified the Pope of the day as the Antichrist and was the first in a long line – which included John Calvin, John Knox, the American Cotton Mather and even Thomas Cranmer, Henry VIII's generally moderate Archbishop of Canterbury – to do so. This has continued down the centuries: in 1988 Ian Paisley claimed Pope John Paul II was the Antichrist and a quick Google search will reveal the 'evidence' of the demonic status of anyone who has occupied the Vatican. Popes regularly die or abdicate, their successor becomes 'Antichrist', the world continues.

The Protestants didn't have it all their own way. The prophecies of the French Catholic Nostradamus (1555) were incredibly popular (and profitable). He, however, identified the Antichrist with the Muslim leader of the Ottoman forces, then threatening southern Europe.

His prophecies are, like those of St John, couched in cryptic terms and lacking any specific dates so they can be tweaked to apply to almost any momentous event.

For centuries, under the influence of a persuasive evangelist, believers have been persuaded to sell their goods (often donating the proceeds to the evangelist), to give up family, friends and home, to gather in some isolated place to await the Rapture, when they will be whizzed up to heaven from where they will look down on the unrighteous in the fires of hell and smugly say, 'I told you so.' The majority have then had to go back to everyday society to deal as best they can with shattered dreams and the amusement of their neighbours, but occasionally there have been less happy outcomes when, rather than be exposed as a fool or a charlatan, the leader has initiated mass suicide. Oddly, the failure of the end of the world to materialise never seems to deter the prophet. He doesn't say he was mistaken, just that he got his calculations wrong. He may recalculate and produce more dates until even the most credulous of the followers have found someone else to follow.

Currently scientists estimate that it will be some 7.5 billion years before the earth finally disappears. But preachers (usually Protestants) regularly pop up saying it will be very soon and only they can save their selected followers.

14. The Diet of Worms Was a Sixteenth-Century Weight-Loss Plan

In 1521 the Holy Roman Emperor Charles V convened a council to which Martin Luther was summoned to answer charges of heresy. This followed the Pope's condemnation of forty-one of his arguments for reform that had been made the previous year. On Luther's refusal to recant his opinions, the Pope excommunicated him. Ordinarily this would have been a virtual death sentence, but Frederick III of Saxony, the ruler of Luther's home state, protected him and requested the hearing. He was one of a group of rulers among the German states who saw this as an opportunity to challenge the Pope's authority.

A Diet (a special council) was held in the town of Worms, an Imperial city which reported directly to the emperor and was the site of a number of assemblies on important political and religious matters, which the Habsburgs regarded as indistinguishable from each other, and whose decisions affected the whole empire. This particular Diet started on 17 April. Luther's journey there was something of a triumphal progress. Towns welcomed him and he took the opportunity to preach in several places. When he appeared Luther again refused to repudiate his writings or his beliefs. Seeing there wasn't much point in going on, the emperor's representative told Luther his views were heretical. The Diet retired to consider its verdict. Seeing how things were going Luther decided to go home. Although he had been given a safe-conduct pass, Charles V issued an edict declaring him an outlaw who could be killed by anyone without fear of the consequences. A fake kidnapping was staged by

Frederick with Luther's knowledge and he was taken to safety.

There was a delay before Charles issued the Diet's formal verdict. He reiterated that Luther was an obstinate outlaw and forbade anyone to help him. His works became forbidden. He went into seclusion in Wartburg Castle, where he began to translate the Bible into German. Although he could not venture out, the events of the Diet were widely reported, spreading his arguments and beliefs far more quickly than he could ever have done by himself. His views received wide support in many of the German states and the emperor was reluctant to get into a confrontation with them. Charles convened the Diet of Speyer in 1526, which was somewhat ambiguously phrased. It seemed to suspend the edict imposed on Luther and even to suggest that the states within the Holy Roman Empire should have religious liberty. This actually led to more Protestant converts, so three years later Charles reimposed the Edict of Worms and cracked the whip over anyone who might be thinking of making up their own mind on such matters.

Luther emerged from hiding, married an ex-nun in 1526 and settled down in Saxony, where he devoted himself to organising new churches, writing hymns and arguing about theological matters. The Diet of Worms, which might have led to a severe loss of weight through Luther being executed or burned at the stake, resulted in fattening the movement he founded and helping it to spread.

15. WITHOUT GUTENBERG, THE REFORMATION WOULD HAVE FAILED

Before 1500 there had been a number of attempts to introduce reforms of the Church, but when copying of documents had to be done slowly, by hand, it was not easy to disseminate ideas. Handwritten translations of the Bible were in circulation, like *samizdat* literature in the Soviet Union, but the number of people who could access them was limited. Preachers' unorthodox beliefs only reached those they could speak to, and the authorities could crush these threats to their power without ideas spreading far.

Then, around 1448, Johannes Gutenberg (1400–68), a goldsmith, invented the printing press. Hundreds of books, pamphlets and single sheets could be produced in a short time. Gutenberg was a good Catholic and his first publication was a Bible. There was no such thing as patents in those days and soon presses flourished all over Europe. Entrepreneurs realised there was also market for romances, mythical stories and even jokes, as well as religious works. This led to increased literacy – there was at last something worth reading and, a bonus, it was relatively cheap to purchase.

There is some dispute about whether Gutenberg was the first to devise printing – other people were experimenting about the same time – but it was an invention whose time had come. Martin Luther himself produced publications and Jean Calvin was a prolific writer. Their followers also took full advantage of this state-of-the-art technology to spread their thoughts, arguments and proposals and the new reading public lapped them up.

16. JEAN CALVIN CREATED A THEOCRACY IN GENEVA

Spelling was not big in the sixteenth century. The child who became famous as Jean Calvin was born in Noyon, France, in 1509, where the name appears as both Jehan Cauvin and Jean Chauvin. His father saw the Church as a good career for his son, so in preparation young Jean studied ancient languages in Paris, but Dad fell out with the local Church and switched the youngster to law. After his father died in 1531, Jean returned to languages, which led him to theology. He began to associate with French reformers and had to go on the run, finding refuge in Switzerland. In 1536 he published his first work of theology in Basel. The combination of religion and law gave Jean the ability to formulate apparently unshakeable arguments. In French his surname means 'bald' so, to avoid taunts of slaphead and worse, he quickly adopted the posher Latin version, Calvinus. The reformer Calvin's convictions were far more fundamentalist than Luther's. He believed in predestination and wanted to do away with hierarchies in the Church to create a more democratic structure of independent congregations who would appoint their own ministers. Ultimately he aimed to establish a theocracy: a state ruled in accordance with his religious principles, where church attendance and Bible studies would be compulsory, and a very sharp eye would be kept on sinners, like people who held private dances in their houses.

On a visit to Geneva Calvin saw the opportunity to start small, undoubtedly hoping that the holy state he created there would be so brilliant that everyone else would want one too. He was offered a job as a teacher in 1538 and immediately tried to persuade the authorities to introduce his fundamentalist plans. He was kicked out.

Three years later he was called back. The city state had descended into political war, but it was not just anarchy that caused this change of heart. A cardinal had proposed returning to Rome, which seemed like a good idea to those who wanted a quiet life, but this alarmed the Protestants. Plus Calvin had some sensible ideas about refuse collection, which was badly needed. Nevertheless, the town council retained the right to reject pastors and teachers, specified some of the pastors' duties and restricted their ability to excommunicate. Calvin managed to get taverns replaced by cafés, where there would be no singing, grace would be said before meals and a Bible would always be available. Customers stayed away in droves, so the taverns were reopened by the council, who needed the tax revenue.

Selling Geneva as a place ruled on strict Calvinist principles, however, brought business to the town, especially the education of nonconformist ministers. During times of persecution in their homelands, Protestants would also take refuge here. All these students and migrants brought prosperity. It even became a sartorial fashion centre: many students adopted a distinctive style of neckwear, known as Geneva bands, which they took back to their homelands. Even if he didn't create a theocracy, Calvin set a fashion.

17. Calvinists Are Tulip Fans

While adhering to the five fundamental principles of all Protestant denominations, those following Calvin have five additional tenets that mark them out. They are summarised by the acrostic TULIP.

Total Depravity is the belief that the Original Sin of Adam and Eve affects every aspect of a person so that everyone is inherently and completely sinful. Original sin is a concept shared by all Christian denominations. What sets the Calvinists apart is their conviction that everyone is rotten through and through.

Unconditional Election is the belief that God has, for his own unknowable reasons and purposes, decided who will be saved (the Elect) and who is damned.

Limited Atonement is the belief that Jesus Christ could have died for everyone, but did not. His sacrifice was made only for the Elect.

Irresistible Grace is the belief that those selected by God cannot resist salvation. Obedience to God's will is implanted by God in those he has chosen – the Elect – and they are reborn in him. This is consoling to those who fear they might not be among the Elect: their willingness to obey God is evidence they have been saved.

Preservation of the Saints is the belief that those who have been saved by God will remain saved, whatever they might do.

How John Calvin felt about flowers in general remains unknown. Presumably he was okay with the lilies of the field and other blooms mentioned in the Bible, but how he would feel about having his beliefs summarised by something many Dutch people almost worship is worth pondering.

18. Calvin Was as Dangerous an Enemy as the Pope

Miguel Serveto Conesa (1509/1511–53), known as Michael Servetus, was the cleverest man of his age. He was a scientist and physician, the first European to work out how the blood circulates from the heart to the lungs and back to the heart again, replenished by oxygen on the way. He was also a talented cartographer, mathematician, meteorologist and astrologer, and wrote poetry on the side. Had he stuck to these relatively safe occupations he might have had a long and happy career in his native Spain, although all scientific discoveries ran the risk of being deemed heretical. However, he also studied the Bible in its original languages and his questioning mind led him to read books proscribed by the highly active Spanish Catholic Church. While attending the coronation of Charles V in Bologna, he was outraged by the pomp and luxury surrounding the Pope. Prudently, he decided not to return to Spain, but travelled to meet various Protestants and fired off a few anti-Catholic diatribes. Like many highly intelligent people, he lacked emotional intelligence and these writings made no concessions to the political realities in his native land.

There was no going back to a country where the Inquisition was making mincemeat of anyone asking interesting questions, so he completed his medical training in France. On graduation he became a doctor in Vienne and took French citizenship. After rejecting the Catholicism of his upbringing he threw in his lot with the Protestants and started a correspondence with Jean Calvin. So far, so good. Then Servetus published a repudiation of predestination, one of Calvin's core beliefs. Calvin took this badly and one of his friends had Servetus denounced as a heretic. He was arrested by the local Roman Catholic authorities, but managed to escape from prison and set off to Italy. Although he was one of the cleverest men in Europe, he lacked street smarts. He stopped off in Geneva to hear Calvin preach and was arrested and imprisoned. The French Catholics wanted him extradited to face heresy charges there, but instead the Genevan Protestants put him on trial for heresy at Calvin's instigation. Pleading ill health and his importance to the governance of Geneva, Calvin sent his secretary to act as the main prosecutor, but he did meet Servetus, who again demonstrated his deficient social skills by insulting the man who controlled his future. The outcome was a foregone conclusion and Servetus was found guilty of heresy. The authorities consulted all shades of Protestant opinion, from Lutherans to others who disagreed with Calvin. Divided on religion, they were unanimous on one thing: Servetus must go. He was sentenced to death by burning, denied the swifter route of beheading – possibly at Calvin's behest – and the sentence was carried out on top of a pyre of his own books, the final insult to a clever man. Servetus was probably the most high-profile victim of Calvin's control and vindictiveness, and his fate shows that Calvin was as dangerous an enemy as the Pope.

19. Fundamentalism Fails

All fundamentalists, whatever their religion, live, sleep, eat, think and breathe their faith. It becomes their primary identity, both personally and communally; they live and associate as far as possible only with those who share their beliefs. They see the world as sharply divided between good (like themselves) and evil (everyone else). Anyone who does not agree is regarded as not simply mistaken, but actively wicked. There is no argument, their version of the truth is not open for discussion or change, but they are selective about which parts of their holy texts they will comply with. This is true of every religion: Christianity, Islam, Judaism, even secular religions like Marxism, all have their fundamentalist wings. Calvinism, being fundamentalist in inspiration, aimed to create a godly world in which all states would be run on Calvinist lines. Even in the places where its tenets were initially embraced – some Swiss cantons (notably Geneva), Scotland, the Netherlands and parts of America – it remains a footnote, albeit a culturally influential one.

To last for so long and to have become so powerful, the Roman Catholic Church needed to be fairly flexible. Although it trumpeted its claims to be eternal and unchanging, it was very good at quietly adapting to local beliefs and practices as long as these could be given a Christian veneer. Churches were built on old sacred sites and spirits of earth and water were transformed into saints whose relics replaced amulets and lucky charms, though these were also tolerated as long as they could be given a religious explanation. There were always individuals who were more Catholic than the Pope, but generally the Church was extremely accommodating to those who did not challenge its authority. Those who did, like the Cathars and others labelled heretics, were swiftly dealt with. The Lutheran tradition followed this pattern of not enquiring too closely into personal beliefs as long as people turned up for services, paid their dues and didn't say anything embarrassing. They became national churches, with associated power, because they tolerated individual differences. Being a Catholic or a Lutheran is not a full-time job.

The Calvinist wing split and split again, as individuals decided they had the ultimate hotline to God and his plan for humanity and took themselves off with their followers to try to create their own vision of the godly society. Some did succeed in attracting enough believers to make the transition from extremist sect to established denomination, like the Quakers or Baptists. Others failed to grow after the death of a charismatic leader: the Sandemanians, Muggletonians, Hutchinsonians, Brownists and their like are now mainly of interest to family historians and academic historians of religion, along with Shakers, Dunkers and the more than Fifty Shades of Calvinism that sprang from Calvin's original theology. Its emphasis on individual conscience and its totalitarianism led to its failure to spread beyond a few centres.

20. Anabaptists United Lutherans, Calvinists and Catholics

Lutherans, Calvinists and Catholics might not have agreed on much, but they all believed that children who died unbaptised would not be joining their family in the afterlife. Of course, they didn't agree where the unblessed soul would go: the Protestants thought hell and Catholics thought limbo. All sides united in hatred of Anabaptists, a general name for various groups with the belief that babies should not be forced to sign up for something they did not understand. They waited until an individual was an adult and could give informed consent before carrying out a baptism or some other ceremony making the individual part of their Church. In a period of high infant mortality they were held to be condemning their children to what was literally a fate worse than death.

The best known of the early Anabaptists are the Mennonites, followers of the Dutchman Menno Simons (1496–1561). His adherents gathered in small groups, especially in the Netherlands, Switzerland, along the Rhine and in Moravia, living simple lives, studying the Bible and having no dealings with the state or with unbelievers. They were committed to a high standard of morality for their members and saw themselves as a Chosen People, so they were receptive to Calvinist principles but, as the Calvinists thought they were the real and only Chosen People, this provoked conflict. The Mennonites' refusal to deal with the state also failed to endear them to governments who needed bodies to pay taxes, fight in wars and keep bureaucracy going. Everyone hated them.

The Englishman John Smyth (*c.* 1565–1612) was ordained an Anglican priest, but then spent time in the Netherlands where he was convinced by Mennonite arguments about adult baptism. Some groups practised baptism by immersion, which Smyth also favoured. He returned to England where he acquired followers and tried to incorporate them into the Mennonites. In the great Calvinist tradition, however, they wanted their own separate club. They rejected the label Anabaptist and called themselves the Brethren or the Brethren of the Baptised Way. The appellation Baptists was first used by their enemies in 1644, about the time they came round to the idea that just sprinkling water was a bit wussy and total immersion was the only way to salvation, but the name stuck.

Both the Baptists and the Mennonites found life in Europe increasingly hostile – all those children not being given the chance of heaven if they died young, all those taxes not being paid. The Baptists took off for America in the seventeenth century and flourished. The Mennonites hung on a while longer, but realised they were getting nowhere and too many of their leaders were being executed, so off they too went and, in a rare example of brotherly love among Calvinists, joined the followers of the Swiss Jacob Amman, known as the Amish. Today they preserve in America a way of life fossilised in the age in which the movement was created.

21. WILDCARDS 2: UNITARIANS

A small section of the reformers who subjected the Bible to close and questioning scrutiny concluded that Jesus Christ is not divine, though his teachings provide a guide for living honourably. They deny one of the fundamental doctrines of Christianity, the Trinity – the threefold nature of God: Father, Son and Holy Spirit – contending that God is a unity, hence their name, Unitarians. In the 1560s a movement in Poland and that hotbed of toleration Transylvania rejected Christ's divinity and (like some others) also rejected the concepts of hell and original sin.

One of those in England who came to agree with the Unitarian tenets was John Biddle (1595–1662), the clever son of a tailor, who went to Oxford and taught there for a time before becoming headmaster of a school in Gloucester just before the outbreak of the English Civil War in 1641. It was a time of great religious and political ferment, and his belief in applying reason to religion combined with his intellectual arrogance was a recipe for disaster. Well-publicised views on the non-validity of the Trinity combined with insults against those who did not agree with him landed him in jail. He managed to write and publish further works, which found an audience. Oliver Cromwell saved him from execution and exiled him to the Isles of Scilly until 1658, when he came to London. He was only free for four years. In 1662 Charles II reimprisoned him, and he died in Newgate. His example and writings lived on clandestinely. The first congregation in England to call itself Unitarian was founded in London in 1774. The best-known Unitarian in England is the scientist Joseph Priestley (1733–1804), who played a significant role in organising the modern Church. In Britain this denomination did not become legal until 1813. Like the Quakers, Unitarians had influence much greater than their numbers would suggest, unsurprisingly in fields like science, which require intellectual analysis, but also in politics, where their critical thought was applied to society's problems.

Unitarianism has a strong following in America, where it has supplied four presidents (John Adams, John Quincy Adams, Millard Fillmore and William Howard Taft), but its presence there is not, unlike so many other denominations, the result of believers leaving Europe due to persecution. It had its origins there in the 'Great Awakening' of the 1740s, one of the various Calvinist campaigns to reawaken commitment to evangelical religion. American Unitarianism was a reaction against this, from both a belief in rational thought and rejection of the Calvinist tenet of inherent sinfulness, preferring a more optimistic view of human nature.

Today Unitarians have no single creed and do not believe that one person or religious tradition has all the answers. They regard diversity of beliefs and tolerance as fundamental. They are still active in their place of origin, Transylvania in Romania, and have adherents across the globe.

22. THE ORTHODOX CHURCH REMAINED ALOOF

The Orthodox Church (whose headquarters are in Constantinople, today's Istanbul) was the original Christian Church from which the Latin Church (whose headquarters are in Rome) began to split off in 1054. After years of squabbles about clerical celibacy, the authority of the Pope, Purgatory and other points of doctrine, the final, bitter divorce came with the sack of Constantinople by the Pope's forces in 1204. Western and Eastern Christianity separated. The Orthodox lands were so poor that the European nations didn't think it was worthwhile invading and in any case, they were too busy squabbling among themselves for more desirable local territories. The Catholics might not have wanted these countries, but the expanding Ottoman Empire saw them as a bridgehead into Europe. Muslim forces sacked Constantinople in 1453 and occupied Greece and the Balkans. The Orthodox Church was tolerated in these conquered lands but was kept on a tight leash, cut off from communication with Western Christianity and with their Russian co-religionists. The different branches of the Orthodox Church developed into national institutions, affirming and preserving local cultural values in the face of Islam. They did not seek converts – too dangerous when apostates from Islam could be executed along with those who converted them.

The different alphabets, Cyrillic in Russia and the Slavic lands and Greek in Greece, were a further barrier to communication, although the revival of classic Greek in the Renaissance did make contact easier. Martin Luther approved of the Greek Orthodox Church and some of his followers were very keen to establish links, as they regarded some of its beliefs and practices as purer and closer to early Christianity than those of the Catholic Church. A long but intermittent correspondence on doctrinal matters followed. In 1629 the Patriarch of Constantinople published a list of Orthodox beliefs shared with Calvinism, but neither side would give way and finally the Greek Orthodox Church rejected Protestantism. The Greeks remained much closer to Catholicism in doctrinal terms, including prayers for the dead, the worship of saints and veneration of relics, which made any rapport impossible with people who regarded such things as the Devil's work.

In the sixteenth century Russia began to make contact with the West. In 1555 the English established the Muscovy Company to trade with Russia. The tsars of the time regarded Orthodoxy as the superior faith (no surprise there) but, as 'the enemy of my enemy is my friend', saw Protestantism as a potential ally against Catholicism. The English aim was commerce, not theology or military co-operation. Ivan the Terrible was nettled that Elizabeth I was only interested in money. Both sides recognised there was no point discussing religion, so that was another opportunity missed. Orthodox Russia remained more or less isolated from European influence until after the dust from the Reformation had settled.

The Orthodox churches were too isolated from Western Christianity to become involved in its disputes. Their main concern was the relationship with local Islamic rulers, not what was going on in the West from which they had long been divided.

23. THE REFORMATION FRAGMENTED EUROPE

In medieval times, the Roman Catholic Church claimed that Europe was united by its Christian faith and was a theocracy ruled in accordance with the Church's teachings, which gave the clergy, headed by the Pope, ultimate political power. The arrival of the Reformation permanently split Europe. As Protestants could not agree among themselves on matters of faith, Europe remained doomed to be disunited.

This cosy picture of a pre-Luther Garden of Eden is a fiction to which everyone paid lip service while Christian rulers pursued wars against other equally Christian rulers – most notably the Hundred Years War (England v. France, 1337–1453) and the Wars of the the Guelphs and Ghibellines (the papacy v. the Holy Roman Empire, 1075–1122), but including a myriad of other minor conflicts and civil wars. The only thing that united the various European powers was their fear of the spread of Islam. Of course, there were political splits when the Pope backed the wrong team and heresies when his authority was threatened, but enforcers managed to silence the voices raised against the Church's power and spin doctors of the day managed to gloss over them. They even managed to maintain that Europe was united in the true faith during periods when there were two popes, one in Rome and the other in France, always out of step with everyone else.

Protestantism shattered that illusion and exposed it for the fiction it was. European wars, previously about territory alone, were still mainly about territory, but with the added poisonous ingredient of religion.

24. Protestants Burned Images, Catholics Burned Bodies

Protestants said that pictures of saints, relics and other knick-knacks designated 'holy' had no religious validity and there was a danger that ignorant believers would worship the objects themselves rather than what they represented. When they gained power in a location their first move was generally an act of iconoclasm, wrecking the interior of Catholic churches. When Catholics gained power in a location their first move was to execute Protestants, generally by burning.

The reasons for this difference are to be found in the theology of the two sides. Membership of Protestant churches came through acceptance of Christ's sacrifice and what that meant, so people had to understand the tenets of the faith to which they were subscribing. Destroying objects and whitewashing over murals helped worshippers to think about what they were being told. Conversion might be a long process of education.

At the time of the Reformation, membership of the Catholic Church came through baptism, followed by attendance at services and compliance with the Church's practices: belief could come in time. The Church would investigate whether individuals could be persuaded to abjure their previous faith and comply with Catholic requirements. If they could not be convinced or were later found to have lapsed they were handed over to the secular authorities. Most were then burned alive; it was intended as a warning to others who might be tempted to follow them, showing a foretaste of the eternal hell that awaited their heretical souls.

25. THE SPANISH INQUISITION PREVENTED SPAIN FROM BECOMING PROTESTANT

An inquisition was a legal process with the aim of investigating and trying heresy within the Catholic Church. Inquisitions started in twelfth-century France in response to religious movements, particularly the Cathars and Waldensians, but today it is the Spanish Inquisition which has the most fearsome reputation, and the name Torquemada has become a byword for bigoted persecution. Tomás de Torquemada, the Grand Inquisitor, was not the enemy of Protestants (he died in 1498 when Martin Luther was still a good Catholic) but of *Marranos* and *Moriscos*, Jewish and Muslim converts. They were the primary targets because the authorities rightly suspected that many of the conversions imposed on them were not sincere. Torture to extract a confession was permitted and the individuals, at what was often literally the sharp end, had to prove their orthodoxy. If found guilty, they had to perform a public penance, the *auto-da-fé* (act of faith). This act of penitence might be swiftly followed by public execution if it was deemed their repentance was not sincere.

The Catholic Church still maintains it did not execute individuals. They were handed over to secular authorities for punishment by the law of the land – usually death by burning. This denial is somewhat ingenuous – very little happened in a Catholic country without the imprimatur of the Church – but it must have been a comfort to those about to die that it was not their Church that was executing them.

The Reformation did not actually cause a big increase in business. By the time it arrived, people were very aware of what awaited those who questioned the authorities, or even annoyed vindictive neighbours. Torquemada had already expanded his empire by increasing the number of branches from one office to two dozen scattered across Spain, and all these people needed to keep themselves busy to justify their existence – and their perks. Confiscated property and possessions enriched persecutors, initially the Crown, but later the Inquisition itself. Some people suspected of Protestant beliefs were investigated, but comparatively few were actually condemned. The estimated numbers of Protestants executed have varied widely over the centuries, but a rough total of between 1,000 and 1,500 between 1540 and 1700 seems to be a fair guess.

The extent and vindictiveness of the Spanish office has been a persistent theme not only of Protestants but also of French and Italian writers, who used its power for political reasons against Spain. Although the nature of the Inquisition in Spain and the body count of its victims have undoubtedly been exaggerated, few would go so far as one modern historian, who claims that 'the Spanish Inquisition was widely hailed as the best-run, most humane court in Europe'.

After the Napoleonic Wars and the Latin American Wars of Independence, the Spanish Inquisition recognised defeat. It was abolished in 1834. The Inquisition itself continued in the Papal States and survives today, renamed the Congregation for the Doctrine of Faith. Its duties have dramatically dwindled to advising the Pope on theological matters. Torture is banned.

26. MARTIN LUTHER PIONEERED THE HYMN BOOK

Traditional Roman Catholic services resemble a concert: the congregation listens passively while the priest, choir and musicians sing and play the sacred music, although no one claps or throws flowers at the end. Martin Luther, who was keen on audience participation, decided that the congregation should not only understand what was going on but also be included, and he introduced the revolutionary notion that they should sing along.

At the time plainsong was used in churches. It's a single, long, melodic line, difficult to sing without a lot of practice, and at that time most people could not read words, let alone music, so would be unable to follow the notes. So, it is said, Luther not only translated religious texts into the vernacular, but set them to popular tunes of the day, thus creating hymns that could be understood and sung by everyone. One of the tunes to which he set the text beginning 'O Haupt voll Blut und Wunden' ('O sacred head sore wounded') is claimed to be an obscene song sung by soldiers at the Battle of Pavia. This is now denied by scholars, although the tune currently used is actually based on a secular love song first published in 1601 and included in J. S. Bach's *St Matthew Passion*.

One theory is that the misunderstanding comes from Luther's use of *bar form*, a term originally referring not to songs sung in taverns but to the rhyming scheme of a text. He does seem to have used folk melodies, although it seems the majority of his tunes, like the lyrics, were composed by him. It is difficult to prove either way because most songs of the day were not written down, they were genuine folk songs. Educated people saw no point in recording the dirty ditties of common soldiers and other lowlifes.

Luther wanted to wean young people away from love songs and 'carnal things'. He produced the first hymn book, arranged according to the seasons and holy days of the Church's year, using music to embed in ordinary people's minds the theology of their religion. Other Protestants have followed Luther's lead, using or adapting familiar tunes to which new, devout words are set. The Wesley brothers, John and Charles, whose hymns are among the most beloved of English congregations, drew on a variety of respectable sources, like existing Anglican hymns or melodies from oratorios or operas. William Booth, founder of the Salvation Army, thought the Devil should not have all the good tunes and actively encouraged the use of music-hall songs as the basis for hymns.

John Calvin, however, thought music of whatever origin far too fancy and mandated psalms intoned to simple tunes. Originally Calvinists also eschewed instrumental music so congregations sang unaccompanied. In the seventeenth century standards began to relax. Baptists introduced hymns which, along with musical instruments, were gradually adopted by some Presbyterian churches. Today some are even introducing Calvinist rap. John Calvin may be turning, at 45 rpm, in his grave.

27. There Is No Difference Between a Sermon and a Homily

From the beginnings of Christianity, following Christ's Sermon on the Mount, telling people how they ought to live was an important part of the service. Early theologians distinguished between the sermon (from Latin for 'discourse') and the homily (from Greek *homilein*, 'to address'). The first was originally defined as a lecture about theological matters in general with the aim of getting people to change their way of life, and the second an explanation of how a passage of Scripture relates to everyday life to help the listeners live a more Christian life. A bewildering number of different types of lectures to the faithful were identified, ranging from explaining the meaning of passages of Scripture to simply telling them what to do, and at times they seem to have swapped meanings – an indication of how similar they became in practice. In Roman Catholicism taking part in the Mass was the essential part and the sermon/homily was often omitted.

With the Reformation more focus was switched to the sermon. As reformers believe salvation comes through faith alone, not just by taking part in a service, at the start of the Reformation it became vital that people should understand what they were signing up to. Doctrine needed to be explained to them, often at very great length. In the Lutheran tradition, both Communion and the sermon are integral parts of the service and both are equally significant. Very often the sermon is technically a homily: an exposition of a Biblical text. In the Calvinist tradition, hearing the word of God is paramount, more important than the Eucharist. The pulpit is still the most prominent piece of furniture in their churches. Sometimes there was a very large hourglass situated within the preacher's eyeline to remind them there were limits to the congregation's attention span and ability to concentrate. Those worried about the state of their lunch in the oven would not be in the right frame of mind to follow complicated theological arguments about the state of their souls. Here the sermon, often contrasting Protestant and Catholic teaching, was and remains the focus of the service.

Homily or sermon, it was always an important part of Protestant services, but the homily was only made an integral part of the Mass by the Second Vatican Council held between 1962 and 1965. Often in practice it is a sermon, telling people what the Church's stance is on a particular issue. It was determined that in the homily it is Christ not the minister who is speaking to the congregation, so it must be delivered by a consecrated priest. In general Protestants also prefer sermons to be delivered by an ordained minister, but this is not regarded as essential; Methodism in particular has a tradition of lay preachers.

In practice, not that many people can tell the difference between a sermon and a homily. Dictionaries now define them as synonyms. Rule of thumb: if it's a Protestant delivering it, it's a sermon. If a Catholic is doing the honours, it's a homily.

28. Christian II's Bad Manners Lost Sweden

Since medieval times Sweden, Norway and Denmark had formed the Kalmar Union, but Denmark's dominance caused resentment and mutterings of rebellion which occasionally blossomed into action. Following one of these unsuccessful uprisings in 1519, Gustav Vasa (1496–1560), a member of the nobility, took refuge for a time in Lübeck, where he was introduced to Protestantism – then gaining ground in Sweden. As well as genuine intellectual conviction, political motives were a strong element: the wish to distance Sweden from the Holy Roman Empire, to which the Danish king Christian II was connected by marriage.

In 1520 Christian II of Denmark, really fed up with constant irritations from Sweden, invaded. He was determined to teach these people a lesson and the Swedes surrendered after some costly battles. Christian decided that a coronation in Stockholm would show them who was boss. He invited all the nobles and main political players to a celebratory feast. Gustav seems not to have been invited. He may have been peeved to be regarded as too unimportant to attend, but realised his luck when the guests were slaughtered on the grounds that they were traitors or, according to a complicit Catholic archbishop, heretics. Among the massacred were Gustav's father and a nephew. He fled north, evaded his pursuers and gathered support from both Sweden and Norway. His army fought their way south, finally gaining Stockholm in 1523. At that time, the monarch was elected by the nobility and Gustav was rewarded with the top job. This was the beginning of the end for Christian. His slaughter of his guests was regarded as dishonourable and he was hardly Mr Popular in his other territories, where he was imposing heavy taxation to fund his wars. He was deposed from the thrones of Denmark and Norway. A year later a treaty recognising Sweden's independence was signed.

Christian may have been a despot who had been thrown out by his subjects, but he was the brother-in-law of the Holy Roman Emperor, and family is family, so Charles V sent a fleet to support his attempt to win back his thrones. Gustav responded by taxing the Catholic Church's property in Sweden to pay for potential war against their co-religionists. At this time, the Church was the major landowner in the country. Naturally the bishops objected and tried to stir up opposition to him, but this was a tactical error. Seeing that no one was too enthusiastic about all the lazy fatcats who just sat around in monasteries, Gustav issued an ultimatum: he would resign if he was not supported. Debates followed, but the prospect of more battles over the succession and also getting their hands on so much land and property made the outcome predictable: the nobles voted for Gustav, Protestantism and the dissolution of the Swedish monasteries. A formal Reformation began in 1527. The first complete Swedish Bible was published in 1541, the year the country declared itself Lutheran. As elsewhere, translation of the Bible boosted a minority language and literacy, which reinforced nationalism.

29. POLAND'S MONARCHS WERE ENLIGHTENED REALISTS

In 1345 Catholic Poland joined with Lithuania (then pagan) to form a union which also later ruled part of Prussia. It was a linguistically and culturally mixed territory. At the time of the Reformation, Lutheranism was enthusiastically received in the north-west German-speaking areas and spread into northern Poland and Lithuania. King Sigismund I (1467–1548), a Catholic, issued his first edict against 'religious novelties' in 1520, but he was consistently unable to impose it or any of his subsequent anti-Protestant decrees. The sheer size of his realm made centralised control problematic. It was landowners who had most local authority and to Sigismund's dismay Calvinism made many converts among them. They largely let their peasants do their own Catholic or Orthodox thing, but sheltered a number of Protestant intellectuals, including exiled Italians, whose ideas were disseminated. To this mix were added about a quarter of a million Jews – refugees from persecution in Germany, Moravia and Bohemia where reform was creating religious paranoia. In 1569 Polish control was extended eastwards to Belarus and parts of the Ukraine, where the Russian Orthodox Church was strong and the population looked to Moscow for religious guidance.

Sigismund was interested in the ideas of the Renaissance and in his reign the arts and sciences flourished. His son, Sigismund II (1520–72), was astonishingly broad-minded for the time. Although a Catholic, in 1556 he recalled a prominent exiled Calvinist reformer, Jan Łaski (1456–1560), to his court. Łaski was from a military Polish family with connections to the Polish court. He had spent time in England, where he was extremely influential, but fled following the accession of the Catholic Mary I. On his return to Sigismund's court he put forward a plan to create a Polish national Church, which would unite all Christian denominations including the Orthodox. Sigismund thought this was a good idea and sent an envoy to the Pope. Though obviously an intelligent and sensible man, the king's decision displayed a somewhat unrealistic grasp of contemporary politics. There was no way that the Pope would accept anything other than complete submission to Catholicism, Calvin's followers brooked no opposition and the Orthodox patriarchs would not have surrendered any control either.

A group of Calvinist scholars, including Łaski, published a Polish translation of the Bible in 1563. In 1565 the Crown accepted the need for religious diversity and abolished state enforcement of Catholic Church jurisdiction. Although this weakened the Church's control, the monarchs remained Catholic and there was no appropriation of Church property, as happened elsewhere. This provided a foundation for the Counter-Reformation to rebuild allegiance and, later, a national identity in opposition to Protestant Germany in the west, the Orthodox states to the east and to communism in the twentieth century.

30. Henry VIII Wanted to Divorce Catherine of Aragon

The daughter of Ferdinand and Isabella of Spain, Catherine of Aragon was six years older than Henry and had been his elder brother Arthur's wife for just six months when she became a widow. Her father-in-law wanted to keep links with Spain and Henry was keen too, but the Church said it was forbidden to marry a brother's widow. Catherine swore that the marriage had never been consummated, Arthur being too sickly to be up for the task, so she had never in truth been his wife. The Pope readily granted a dispensation and the marriage went ahead in 1509. But fourteen years later Catherine had had six pregnancies, five of which resulted in stillborn children or children who lived for only a few days. Only one of the couple's offspring, their daughter Mary, survived. Henry was desperate for a son and Anne Boleyn, the sister of a former mistress, caught his eye. Like many men, Henry decided to trade in his old wife for someone younger and prettier – and, he hoped, capable of bearing healthy children.

At first it seemed a fairly simple matter. Usually the Pope readily granted dispensations to the rich and powerful. Although divorce was the word used at the time and has been ever since, Henry was actually seeking an annulment of his marriage to his wife. He wanted the Pope to declare it had never been a valid marriage and so he had always been a single man and could marry Anne Boleyn.

In 1527 Henry started negotiations. These dragged on for six long years. Henry could not understand it. He saw other kings dispose of unwanted wives with relative ease. Some women gracefully agreed to enter a convent, others were forced to accede to a hitherto unregarded point of Church law. Given the intermarriages among the royal families of Europe, a forbidden degree of relationship could usually be unearthed. However, at the time the Papal States were under the control of the King of Spain, Charles V, and Catherine was his aunt. She wasn't going to go quietly and Charles wasn't going to have her disrespected or his cousin Mary called a bastard. So the Pope said no. When Anne became pregnant in 1532 – either by accident or in a planned move – the matter became urgent. As his Protestant advisers suggested, the only way Henry would be able to end his marriage was by appointing a sympathetic Archbishop of Canterbury and declaring himself head of the Church. This would mean making England a Protestant state, which was their ultimate agenda. Anne herself was sympathetic to Protestantism, but in her position she needed to be. Although at heart a Catholic who would have happily remained a good son of the Church if he had been given his own way, Henry set in train the events that would expel Catholicism from England. He declared himself Supreme Head of the Church of England in 1534 and started to dismantle the infrastructure of the Roman Catholic Church that had thwarted his desires.

31. BECOMING A PROTESTANT WAS A CAREER MOVE FOR ANNE BOLEYN

Anne Boleyn's father, Thomas, was a man on the make at the court of Henry VIII. A diplomat fluent in French, he used his contacts to get his two daughters into the French court, even then regarded as a kind of finishing school for well-bred girls looking to marry well. Mary, the elder, had a fling with King François I and was packed off in disgrace. Anne, who followed her sister to Frouce in 1514 aged about thirteen, was more streetwise. She entered the household of François's wife, the intensely pious Claude, and quickly became a favourite. She played the lute and danced well, was a witty conversationalist in French and must have convinced Claude of her Catholic credentials. After her return to England in 1522, her sophistication made her the It Girl of the day. She caught Henry VIII's eye and he became obsessed, precipitating the break with Rome which created the Church of England. Her support for reform has often been interpreted as a political move: becoming Protestant was the only way she could ensnare the king into marriage.

This is the usual story, but Anne's interest in reform actually started while she was in the French court a long time before she met the King of England. Here she acquired a number of books condemned by the Catholic Church. These weren't the sixteenth-century equivalent of the books which people buy as intellectual fashion statements to impress their friends: she actually read them. Nor was Henry in her sights. Her father called her back to England to marry James Butler, the son of a relative with whom he had a dispute, in order to resolve this family problem.

But the match didn't come off. Next, Anne secretly became engaged to Henry Percy, son of the Earl of Northumberland, in what was probably a love match. Cardinal Wolsey had other plans for the lad, however, and Anne was on the rebound when Henry joined the pack pursuing this clever, fascinating, fashionable woman. He outranked all the others and could make life extremely disagreeable for anyone who crossed him, but Anne held him at arm's length, tantalising him for six years. Probably her decision to then sleep with the king and become pregnant was a strategic political move, possibly prompted by religious opportunism because she saw an chance to further the cause of reform.

After marriage she remained close to evangelical preachers and writers, even using her influence with the king to rescue a French poet imprisoned for his beliefs, whom she brought to England and appointed tutor to the sons of her sister. She also encouraged other rising stars of what became the Protestant movement. During her final days, just three years after her marriage, she heard the Catholic Mass and, although she was not accompanied to the scaffold by a priest, it seems she never left the Catholic Church to become a fully fledged Protestant. She was of the party that wanted reform, not to start a new denomination.

32. THOMAS MORE WAS NOT A NICE MAN

Thomas More, the English lawyer and statesman, has gone down in history as a gentle saint, canonised in 1935 and in 2000 made patron saint of statesmen and politicians. He is even remembered in the Church of England as a martyr. Famous as part of a circle of humanist scholars, More's best-known work is *Utopia* (Greek for 'nowhere'), a novel describing an ideal society, published 1516. Its title has become a synonym for any plan to reform society, albeit an unrealistic one. He became Henry VIII's Chancellor in 1529. More saw this appointment as a chance to continue the campaign to eradicate heresy from England. He was violently anti-Reformation, but this was possibly the worst time to accept such a sensitive post. The king was seeking to have his marriage to Catherine of Aragon annulled and when this failed he declared himself head of the Church of England. More's beliefs did not allow him to acknowledge this. He offered his resignation, which was finally accepted, but Henry would not leave him in peace: he wanted this celebrated man's endorsement of his actions. Following his refusal to deny papal supremacy and to accept the annulment of Henry's first marriage, More was subjected to a show trial, found guilty and executed.

Close reading of *Utopia*, however, reveals an obnoxious society. Utopia's more attractive features include social services that were only gradually achieved in Britain from the nineteenth century onwards, such as free state education, universal adult suffrage, a basic state income for the working class, a national health service and the ordination of women. A six-hour working day remains an unrealised hope and the religious toleration in the novel was something More himself strenuously campaigned against. In return for these benefits, the inhabitants of Utopia were not allowed to make up their own minds on what work they wanted to do and or when they would do it. Even their leisure time was strictly regulated. They were not allowed to go to pubs or wine bars, to brothels or to meet in secret. Discussion of government policy without permission was a capital offence. It's the kind of totalitarian state that is not disimilar to some twentieth-century regimes.

Utopia was written before the upheaval of the Reformation, which began in 1517. As the Reformation built up a serious head of steam, More wrote a series of extensive refutations of Luther's teachings and defences of Catholic doctrine, both at Henry's behest and on his own initiative. As Chancellor he ordered the full implementation of medieval heresy laws, which had largely fallen into disuse. He was particularly keen to censor publications and burned both books and bodies. In this he was a man of his times, but it is a long way from the popular view of him as a devoted family man who died for his principles. He might be better commemorated as the patron saint of dictators.

33. Monks, Friars and Nuns Were Thrown Penniless onto the Streets During the Dissolution of the Monasteries

Between 1524 and 1528, while Henry VIII was still an obedient son of the Catholic Church, some thirty religious houses in England and Wales were closed by Cardinal Wolsey because they were simply not viable. The substantial money released was mainly used to found educational establishments. These profits may have been Henry's inspiration, in 1534, to commission a survey of the property of religious houses in England and Wales, and at the same time conduct another survey to see how well the inhabitants were complying with his demand to be recognised as Supreme Head of the Church in England. Undoubtedly the findings were carefully edited to suit his purposes, but many abuses were found. This was not entirely propaganda, as similar findings were being made in other countries. The results gave him the grounds to carry out the so-called Dissolution of the Monasteries.

Between 1536 and 1541 over 850 religious houses in England and Wales were disbanded, starting with the smaller communities and moving on to the largest. The aim was partly to reduce the power of the Roman Catholic Church, but mainly to profit from their possessions. It is estimated that the larger and richer establishments owned one-third of the land. This, along with valuables like gold, silver and lead, were appropriated by the Crown. This resulted in around 12,000 individuals (7,000 monks and friars, 3,000 canons and 2,000 nuns) being ejected from their institutions. A few of those who strongly resisted were executed. Some, those with a true vocation, went abroad to enter other religious houses of their orders. Others were able to find positions in ordinary churches, but the majority were given adequate pensions. It was the lay people who did most of the actual work in these establishments who were left unemployed with no pay-offs.

In 1540, the exercise was repeated in Ireland. The situation here was different. The king only effectively ruled a small area around Dublin, known as the Pale, where there was little opposition. Outside it, the local chieftains and warlords were in control. They presented more resistance to dissolution than in England, but the offer of the monastic lands and benefits in return for swearing allegiance to the English crown persuaded some to comply. It was a long process: at Henry's death in 1547 only about half the religious houses had been closed, but here too those who went willingly received pensions. Those in Ireland who wanted to remain within the Catholic religious life seem to have been offered shelter in the households of chieftains who were effectively beyond English control. It was not until 1649, under Oliver Cromwell, that the last few monastic buildings in the far west were destroyed.

In Scotland there was no formal programme of dissolution. As the Presbyterians increased their influence and control in the wider society, no new applicants to monasteries or convents appeared. The religious houses here were just left to wither away without creating either martyrs, homeless beggars or a need to pay pensions.

34. The Dissolution of the Monasteries Damaged Children's Health

A recent article by Benjamin Penny-Mason on archaeological evidence from skeletons shows that during the reign of Henry VII (1485–1509), which ended the Wars of the Roses and brought stability to England, children were significantly healthier than in the period after the Reformation. Damage peaked in 1540, perhaps because monasteries and convents provided support for the poor and ill. But there are other possibilities. The fourfold increase in rickets, caused by lack of Vitamin D, might be due to inadequate food, but the fashion for wrapping children in swaddling bands designed to straighten their bones meant their bodies were not much exposed to sunlight, which is also necessary for good bone development.

It wasn't all bad, however: their teeth improved, for reasons which have still to be investigated. The 1530s were also a period of economic and social problems. A rising population, a succession of bad harvests and prolonged poor weather led to an increase in prices resulting in a significant increase in the number of impoverished people, some of whose employment prospects went with the religious houses. There was even famine in some places. Although an Act of 1536 obliged the Anglican parish to collect voluntary contributions to look after those unable to care for themselves, it took some time before a proper system could be implemented. All that can be said at the moment is that the destruction of the Church's support system contributed to ill health in the most vulnerable section of society.

35. HENRY VIII'S REFORMS CAUSED MASSIVE POPULAR UPRISINGS AMONG CATHOLICS

In October 1536 a protest in Louth, Lincolnshire, against the closure of its local abbey and other religious houses soon spread to nearby towns. It was quickly defused by the threat of military intervention. Two of the leaders and a number of others involved were captured and hanged at Tyburn. Twelve days later a rising in Yorkshire presented a far more serious problem to the authorities. The various rebellions at this time are usually lumped together as the Pilgrimage of Grace, although it is just this uprising that should be given the title. Led by Robert Aske and under banners depicting the Five Wounds of Christ, some 9,000 men occupied York. They reinstated monks and nuns there, driving out those who had moved in and restored full Catholic services. Gathering support from other northern counties, they moved on to Hull and Pontefract, where they occupied the castle. Up to 40,000 assembled in Doncaster where Aske met representatives of the king. One of them, the Duke of Norfolk, promised them a general pardon, that Parliament would meet in York and that the religious houses would be reprieved until this meeting. They believed him (never a good move with monarchs and their servants) and dispersed.

But Norfolk did not have the king's authority to make these pledges; he was massively outnumbered by the rebels and mainly intended to save his skin, although as a Catholic he must have sympathised. Aske travelled to London to meet the king, who temporised to buy time, suggesting he might accede to their demands. Then in February of the following year a further uprising took place, this time across Cumberland and Westmoreland, led by a Yorkshire knight, Sir Francis Bigod. Putting this down also gave Henry the excuse to declare martial law and pursue the Yorkshiremen as well. Fifteen of the leaders were given a show trial and executed. Several hundred of their followers were also executed.

Although primarily for religious reasons, and often represented as a sign of the strength of allegiance to Catholicism in England, these rebellions had more than one cause. They followed a bad harvest in 1535, which had been better in the West Country, where there was no uprising, and another in 1536 which was also disappointing. There were other economic and political factors and Henry did concede a few of the demands, like delaying the collection of some taxes and modifying a law. He established a court, the Northern Council, to visit the major towns so people would not have to travel so often to London. Some compromises on religious matters were made, although not the dissolution of the monasteries. The rebellions were actually used as an excuse to speed up their suppression. There were no uprisings elsewhere, which suggests that local issues were driving the northern events.

The comparative ease with which Henry defused the situation implies that the religious element was not the sole or even the major reason for the uprisings: people are prepared to die for their religion, but no one has ever died for a tax cut.

36. PROTESTANTISM TRANSFORMED THE LANDSCAPE

It was not just the suppression of the monasteries, their destruction or conversion to other uses that changed the landscape in Protestant countries. A more profound difference was produced by the sweeping away of smaller and more personal landmarks. These can still be seen in parts of Catholic Europe, showing how Protestant landscapes once looked.

Although St Christopher is the official saint for travellers, St Botolph was the preferred local boy in England. As well as the many churches dedicated to him, there would have been spots at crossroads where the lost, in the absence of a signpost, could pray for divine assistance to take the right route. Wayside shrines were not just for travellers. Others might be dedicated to saints, believed to have powers to help when invoked for a particular cause, like finding (or getting rid of) a husband.

Small chapels were often located at places of pre-Christian pagan importance, like bridges where water spirits were venerated. All over the country were wells whose waters were believed to have miraculous powers. Undoubtedly these were pagan sites, but the Church appropriated them and attached a legend (usually fictitious) of a Christian saint to them. Crosses, shrines and chapels can be smashed, but it is more difficult to get rid of a well. So important were these holy wells that, long after the Reformation, they remained locally potent, often the focus of well-dressing festivals. They survived longest in the Celtic fringes of Wales, Cornwall, Ireland and Scotland. This was partly because of the power of Celtic mythology, but mainly because these were not considered important regions and were distant from Puritan authorities. Very few holy wells survived in eastern England, where Protestantism was early and firmly established.

Tens of thousands of crosses, not just in churches, were once scattered all over Britain. A few have survived in market places, like the Eleanor crosses erected by Edward I to mark the places where the body of his wife, Eleanor of Castile, rested on the route from Lincoln to London. Those at crossroads had particular significance. In pre-Christian times these were mystical places. Their significance long survived the rationalism of the Reformation: until 1823 they were the site for the burial of suicides.

Even trees might be holy. People would hang objects from the branches, symbolising a benefit they believed they had received. In England it remained common for manorial courts to assemble at an oak tree – although they usually decamped to somewhere more congenial, like the local pub.

For Protestants these wayside crosses, shrines and holy sites were symbols of superstition and idolatry that had to be swept away, and their disappearance probably had a greater psychological effect on ordinary people than the loss of the monasteries. Just as churches became plain and unadorned, the removal of all these little landmarks with their local and personal links was a clear indication of a complete break with the past. Within a short time, an environment which had been suffused with religious symbols was now swept clean. It was not just the physical landscape that was changed, but the mental landscape.

37. Denmark Voted for Protestantism

At the time of the Reformation, Denmark ruled Norway, part of Sweden, Greenland, Iceland, the Faroe Islands, the duchies of Schleswig and Holstein on the German border and the largest island in Estonia. The ruler was elected. This meant kings had to steer a careful course. Although Frederik I of Denmark and Norway (1471–1533) started his reign as a Catholic and swore to exterminate Lutheranism, he recognised the need to conciliate reform views. He ordered his Protestant and Catholic citizens to share the same churches, promoted a Danish bible and even appointed Lutheran tutors to educate his son, Christian.

By the time of Frederik's death in 1534 his realm was well on the way to Protestantism. One faction wanted to reinstate his nephew, Christian II, a hard-line Catholic who had been deposed and exiled by a group of electors in 1523 and replaced with Frederik. The other faction wanted to continue the reforms. The war between them, called the Counts' Feud (1534–6) because it was between noblemen, was more or less on religious grounds. With the support of Gustav Vasa, King of Sweden, the Protestants won and elected Frederik's son, who was crowned as Christian III (1503–59). Having been educated by Protestants, he involved both Martin Luther and the theologian Phillip Melanchthon in order to impose Luther's brand of Protestantism as the state religion in his territories. Protestantism in Scandinavia was chosen by ballot. Doubtless the distribution of Church lands among the electors had no effect on their decision to reject Catholicism.

38. A BOOK OF PROTESTANT THEOLOGY WAS A BESTSELLER IN SIXTEENTH-CENTURY ITALY

As elsewhere, in the Italian states there were many people questioning the Catholic Church's teachings and practices in the sixteenth century. One of these was Don Benedetto of Mantua, a Benedictine monk living in Naples, who wrote *The Benefit of Jesus Christ, Crucified* (known by its short title *Del Beneficio di Cristo*). This was published in the Republic of Venice in the early 1540s, and sold 40,000 copies in the following six years (a sales figure most current academics can only envy). At a time of widespread illiteracy, this was a remarkable number. Written in clear, simple Italian, it was a popular work not only with the laity but with churchmen, and a number of cardinals praised it. However, others attacked it as Lutheran and it was publicly burned in Naples. Heretics hauled before the Inquisition were regularly accused of having read it. However, Don Benedetto was not citing Luther or his followers, although he must have known their works. He just quoted the teachings of early doctors of the Church, like St Augustine, that justification was not by works but by faith, unless accompanied by a pure heart. He also said, like Martin Luther, that the Scriptures were the ultimate guide. Jean Calvin's views on predestination also seem to have been an influence. Don Benedetto died, apparently peacefully in his monastery in the south, around 1544.

The publication was later placed on the Index of Prohibited Books, which Catholics were forbidden to read, created in 1559. It was suppressed so successfully by the Inquisition that it disappeared completely for some 300 years. It is now known from a copy found in St John's College, Cambridge in England, during the nineteenth century. This work encapsulates the fate of Italian Reformers, or indeed anyone who questioned any aspect of the Church or its teachings. If they were lucky, their books were burned. If they were unlucky, like an early critic of corruption, Girolamo Savonarola (1452–98), and numerous others long forgotten, they themselves were burned at the stake.

There were many groups who gathered to discuss and share ideas, but they never managed to come together in one movement. Nor, crucially, did the noble families in Italy support and protect reformers, as happened elsewhere; they depended on the Church for lucrative posts, like those of bishop and cardinal, from which came their power. No one was willing to jeopardise their family fortunes for some obscure preacher's notions. The fate that awaited those who fell foul of the Inquisition or the Index meant that most budding reformers either recanted or fled the country to go to Germany, Poland, Switzerland or even England, where they and their writings stood a better chance of survival. Some joined the Waldensians in their settlements in the Alpine valley in Piedmont, then under the rule of the Duke of Savoy. Despite this reformist bestseller, by about 1600 Protestantism was effectively wiped out in the Italian states.

39. Edward VI's Reign Was the Turning Point in England

Edward VI (1537–53) came to the throne in 1547 at the age of nine, on the death of his father, Henry VIII. His father stipulated a council to act as collective regent while the boy was still too young to rule himself, but his mother's brother Edward Seymour, Duke of Somerset, soon managed to seize sole power, calling himself Protector. Edward VI was given a Protestant upbringing and by the age of eleven had argued that the Pope was the Biblical Antichrist. He was also keen on hearing sermons. His diary, kept for two years from 1550, suggests that, like many teenagers, he thought he had all the answers and firmly told people where they went wrong. He lectured his elder sister Mary about her Catholicism and disapproved of her dancing and having a laugh.

Such a young monarch inevitably attracted a power struggle for control. Initially, this was between his uncles, Protector Somerset and Thomas Seymour, who was also the husband of his stepmother Catherine Parr. Both uncles were executed – something of an occupational hazard for Tudor nobility. Thomas met his end in 1549 at the instigation of his brother Somerset, who himself was soon under threat, accused of abuses of power. He took the young king as a kind of hostage, but was captured and imprisoned. John Dudley, Duke of Northumberland, replaced him as head of the council. Three years later Edward laconically recorded his uncle's death: 'The duke of Somerset had his head cut off upon Tower Hill between eight and nine o'clock in the morning.' The diary reveals a guarded and detached individual, which is understandable considering the machinations of those around him and the possible threats to himself.

Whatever their differences, both Somerset and Northumberland pursued reform policies which laid the foundations of a Protestant state. The only person Edward himself really trusted was Thomas Cranmer, Archbishop of Canterbury, who strongly influenced him. Cranmer was able to introduce the reforms that created the Church of England we know today; the most important for the average churchgoer was his revision of the Book of Common Prayer – for centuries the loved cornerstone of Anglican worship – but Cranmer's formulation of forty-two articles of faith (later reduced to thirty-nine) defined the distinctive theology of the Church of England. It was also under Edward VI that chantries were finally abolished. These trust funds had been set up by the wealthy to pay for a stipulated number of masses to be sung by a Catholic priest in order to reduce the time spent in Purgatory by their souls or the souls of those they loved. This elimination swept away the last remnants of Catholic institutions in England that had begun with his father's dissolution of the monasteries.

Although Edward VI, like his sister Mary I, looks like an intermission between the dramatic break of Henry VIII and the legacy of Elizabeth I, it was in his brief reign that the foundations were laid for the ultimate success of moderate Protestantism in England.

40. Thomas Cranmer Wrote the Book of Common Prayer

Roman Catholic religious services were contained in a number of books. The most frequently used were the *Missal*, giving the various masses to be celebrated throughout the church year, and the *Breviary*, containing prayers, Biblical readings, hymns, etc., used by those conducting services. In addition the *Manual* contained occasional services, like baptism, marriage, burial and the like, and the *Pontifical* detailed services conducted by bishops. Music used in worship was laid down in two further handbooks. All were in Latin and incomprehensible to the average man or woman in the pew.

When the Reformation arrived, the first step was to translate the Latin texts into English. Work on translating the Bible had thrown up numerous errors in the Latin used by the Catholic Church. It would not be a simple matter. Theologically acceptable alternatives had to be found. Thomas Cranmer, Henry VIII's Archbishop of Canterbury, began a cautious adaptation of a Latin translation, incorporating Martin Luther's Litany and passages from Miles Coverdale's translation of the Bible published in 1544.

Under Edward VI, Cranmer went on developing services that would reflect the new beliefs. Keeping up with changes was not an easy matter. In 1549 the first edition of the *Book of Common Prayer* for the Church of England was published. Cranmer had drawn together all the important services of the Anglican Church into a single volume that could be easily read by the literate and understood by everyone. His language was inclusive. Most of the words used are of English origin, which have more emotional power than the Latin of the elite or the Norman French of the law. Many of the phrases in the BCP come in pairs: one word speaking to the educated and the second to those who could not even sign their names. 'We have erred and strayed' where 'err' from the Latin *errare* gave the university-educated lord a feeling of superiority and 'stray' with Old English roots was familiar to an agricultural labourer with wayward sheep. It was always intended as a stopgap. Revisions removed more and more words and concepts regarded as too Catholic and another edition was published in 1552, the year before Mary I's accession and her attempt to return the country to Catholicism. Cranmer was burned at the stake, not because of his authorship of the BCP, but because of his Protestantism. After his death, amendments went on being made.

Under Elizabeth I, a cautious path was picked between conservative Anglicans and Puritan reformers. In 1559 another revision was published and this version lasted until Elizabeth's death. Her successor, James I, brought up in Presbyterian Scotland, found it too Catholic. His successor Charles I found it not Catholic enough. The Commonwealth (1642–60) attempted to get rid of it altogether. It was not until 1662 that the final version, retaining much of Cranmer's original elegant prose but not his original version, was produced largely by Anglican bishops and clergy. It remained in use until the late twentieth century.

41. THE REFORMATION HAD NO EFFECT ON THE CATHOLIC CHURCH

The Catholic Church was somewhat shattered by the unquenchable enthusiasm aroused by Protestantism. Like any multinational business facing a competitor, its first response to a threat was to propose a committee. The idea was rejected by key players of all persuasions, Catholic and Protestant. Eventually the Council of Trent met for the first time in 1545. Protestants were invited to attend but told they could not vote. This seemed pointless, so it comprised only Catholic delegates, although it called itself ecumenical.

Not all popes or other Catholic power brokers, like the French king, supported the council, and more pressing matters like wars intervened, so over the next eighteen years it met only intermittently. Finally, in 1563, it issued its proposals. It concluded that the Catholic Church should not argue with Protestants on their own ground but should market itself better by accentuating what it already did.

The outcomes were primarily to condemn Protestantism and restate all the teachings Protestants criticised as without Biblical sanction, such as transubstantiation, the invocation of saints, veneration of relics, justification by works and other traditional practices. But it did crack down on abuses, such as the sale of indulgences, the practice that had kicked off the whole Reformation. The council also recommended an overhaul in administration to improve the morals in religious houses and the education of the clergy, whose suitability and morals had to be supervised by their bishop. It also said that bishops live in their diocese and not be allowed to collect benefices to bring in a good income while delegating the work to a poorly paid substitute or neglecting it altogether. Priests too had to reside in their parish. They also forbade duelling on pain of excommunication, which seems to have had little effect.

The sacred books of the Church, including the Vulgate Bible, the Breviary and the Missal, were to be overhauled. The place of and kind of music used in the Church needed clarification. Perhaps the most important and lasting results were the issue in 1565 of the Tridentine Mass (in Latin), used for the next 400 years, and the Roman Catechism, the statement of the Church's fundamental beliefs.

The campaign that resulted from this restatement of the doctrines and practices of the Church lasted until around 1650, and is known as the Counter-Reformation, the Catholic Revival or the Catholic Reformation. The first two terms seem a more accurate description of the Council's outcome as there was no substantive reform, simply an improvement in how the Church was conducted. Most of the abuses exposed by the reformers were acknowledged and the revision of the holy books used by the Church produced standardised texts, making practice more uniform across Europe. By making the Church look more closely at what it did reformers did achieve some changes, but because the basic beliefs were reiterated there was no possibility of reaching accommodation or of preventing a split.

42. Bloody Mary Was Bloody Unlucky

The only surviving child of Henry VIII and his first wife, Catherine of Aragon, Mary I (1516–1558) came to the English throne after the death of her younger brother, Edward VI, in 1553. On his deathbed her brother had tried to disbar her from the succession because she was a Catholic, but this was regarded as unfair and she received massive popular support despite her religion. Looking back, Mary seems like a hiatus in the steady march of England on the route to Protestantism, sandwiched between Edward VI and Elizabeth I, but at the time things were a lot less certain. Outside the south-east and among the majority of the population there was no widespread ideological commitment to the new religion. The relatively few people who were prepared to fight for it were those who actually cared or those who profited from the new religion, like the beneficiaries of the Dissolution of the Monasteries. They were matched by those who genuinely wanted to restore the old faith. The majority would probably have gone along with whichever side won, so at the beginning of Mary's reign Protestantism had only a tenuous hold.

Her failure to reimpose Catholicism resulted from several factors. The first was her inability to produce a child. Her husband, Philip, the heir to the Spanish throne, readily admitted he had married her for political reasons and spent as little time in the country as he could decently manage. After two phantom pregnancies Mary had to accept that there would be no child to succeed her.

Mary also threw away her initial support through her determination to reimpose Catholicism by strong-arm methods: burning heretics at the stake. Her zeal earned her the nickname Bloody Mary. Even her Spanish husband thought this a bit excessive and advised her to go easy, but she would not listen and this campaign further stoked fear and resentment against her religion. Marrying a foreigner whose country was seen as a threat to England's overseas trade and growing power in the world was not popular either. The Spanish refused to share the profits of their lucrative ventures in South America, but Philip demanded money from her to pursue his war against the French, with whom the English had good trading relations. Also under Mary's rule, England lost its last outpost in France, the town of Calais. England had long claimed French territories and this was a symbolic as well as an economic blow.

Mary was not just unwise in how she dealt with the religious, commercial and political problems of her reign, she was very unlucky in a peculiarly British way. Her reign coincided with a period of excessive rainfall, resulting in bad harvests and famine in parts of the country. In the days before accurate weather forecasting, this was seen as a sign of God's displeasure, and this further stroke of misfortune may have been the final nail in the coffin of her hopes to restore Catholicism in England.

43. THE BRITISH DON'T LIKE MARTYRS

In England no one actually took up arms in a war of religion, although the English Civil War had religious aspects. As far as can be determined, over 373 Protestants and more than 200 Catholics died in England and Wales between 1534 and 1680, but over 1,000 perished in Ireland between 1540 and 1714. Some of those included died in prison before trial and others were found guilty posthumously. The link between religion and politics also makes it difficult to determine who died for their religious beliefs and who for political acts. Records in Ireland were either not kept or have not survived, making figures here particularly difficult to compile. In Scotland during the Reformation, twenty-two (or by some estimates twenty-four) Protestants were executed, one was assassinated and two others suffered non-capital punishment. Four Catholic churchmen (one of them doubtful) were executed, but no laymen or women.

Both Catholics and Protestants insisted that people were executed after a due process of law. In Catholic states holding heretical opinions was a capital offence. Under Mary I, immortalised in English history as Bloody Mary, over 300 Protestants died. It was not just Catholic Mary who executed Protestants. Between 1536 and 1680, seventy-three men and women were executed for being the wrong kind of Protestant under Henry VIII, Edward VI, Elizabeth I and James I. Their stories, along with others dating back to the medieval Lollards and including deaths in Scotland, were collected by John Foxe and published in his *Actes and Monuments* (1563), known as *Foxe's Book of Martyrs*, which had a forceful anti-Catholic influence for centuries. From 1571 a copy was kept in cathedrals, some churches and other religious establishments.

Catholics were also executed for legal reasons, but this was under the treason laws, like those who refused to accept Henry VIII or Edward VI as head of the Church in England. In the first twelve years of Elizabeth I's reign no Catholics were executed. Then in 1570 Pope Pius V excommunicated her. This was not a sensible move, since it transformed every Catholic into a potential terrorist as they owed their ultimate allegiance to a foreign power. Priests who were caught in England and Wales became automatically regarded as agents of an enemy state and were executed. Most Catholics in England were loyal to the throne, but suffered extreme repression because they were lumped in with those who did decide to plot to replace Elizabeth with a Catholic.

Although it was no consolation to those who did pay the ultimate price for their faith, whether Catholic or Protestant, British people got off comparatively lightly during the Reformation. Some 200,000 died during the Wars of the Three Kingdoms (1639–51) in the British Isles. Although the Scottish and Irish wars were based on religion, the English Civil War was primarily political. Up to 400,000 people died in the French Wars of Religion (1562–98). The Thirty Years War (1618–48) saw off between 3 million and 11.5 million souls. Even in Spain, where there was no religious war, over 1,000 people were executed as heretics.

44. Elizabeth I Was a Weak and Feeble Woman

That was certainly the opinion of the men around her. Although there have been suggestions that she was a man in drag, her ladies-in-waiting would have noticed this. When she came to the throne in 1558 her position was certainly weak. The House of Commons had a strong Puritan faction, while the Lords still had Catholic bishops and members of the nobility. But she was never feeble. Steering her way between these extremes to get legislation passed was an arduous process. She also had to resist attempts to marry her off to someone who would, according to the customs of the day, dominate her. Elizabeth I was probably the most intelligent monarch England ever had, although it's not a strongly contested title. Her own religious views were moderate. She said there was one God, one Christ and the rest was a dispute about trifles. Nor did she want to 'open windows into men's souls'. Although a Protestant, she protected Catholics in her employ. She used the female stereotype of the day to manipulate her advisers by flirting, losing her temper, changing her mind and delaying making decisions. It drove the men around her mad, but by the end of her reign in 1603 she had established a moderate Church of England, which has lasted to the present day. As the first successful female on the throne of England, who created a stable, prosperous and culturally vibrant state, she also proved that a woman could succeed in the macho world of international politics.

45. FRANCE MIGHT HAVE BECOME A PROTESTANT COUNTRY

No one who was anyone in France in the early sixteenth century disputed that the Catholic Church needed reform, and many peasants were of the same opinion, although their opinion didn't much matter. Initially, Martin Luther's brand of moderate reform appealed, but soon followers of the more radical Swiss Huldrich Zwingli emerged. In 1534 the king, François I, woke to find a Protestant placard of the Zwinglian persuasion pasted to his own bedroom door. This was insupportable. Previously attempting to steer a course between Catholics and reformers, he now took a harder line on heresy. An increase in prosecutions and executions followed, but in vain. When Frenchman Jean Calvin began to publish theological works from Basel, and later Geneva in Switzerland where he had taken refuge, many of his compatriots were converted to his beliefs. Missionaries also came from Switzerland to spread the Calvinist word. They had the most success south of the Loire, but Normandy in the north became another stronghold. It is currently estimated that about 12 per cent of the population were Protestants by 1570. This was by no means a threat to the government at that time, and is probably comparable to the figure of genuine believers in England in 1534 when Henry VIII imposed his form of Protestantism. However, the monarchy and the Pope were panicked by the growth of such strident protest.

The conflict was triggered in 1562 when armed men accompanying the Duke of Guise (from the leaders of the strongly Catholic faction in court) fired on and killed many worshippers in a Huguenot congregation in Vassy. The duke claimed he had been pelted with stones by the Huguenots and on his return to Paris was given a hero's welcome. Protestants retaliated by seizing a number of key towns and warfare broke out.

In the years that followed nine Wars of Religion are differentiated, each concluded by a treaty which offered limited toleration to Protestants, but this was in fact one long conflict, punctuated by truces in which the combatants regrouped and rearmed themselves. Inevitably the other European powers were drawn in because of France's prominence on the Continent, and equally inevitably both sides behaved appallingly. Finally, in 1598, the Edict of Nantes, giving Protestants restricted rights, was issued by Henri IV. He had been raised a Protestant, but in 1589 was given an ultimatum: convert to Catholicism or forego the throne. Famously, he is said to have given a Gallic shrug, replied, 'Paris is worth a Mass' and acceded.

An uneasy peace remained, with Protestantism making many converts until 1685, when Louis XIV revoked the Edict and outlawed Protestantism. Up to a quarter of a million fled abroad and those that remained went underground or converted.

France might have been happier as a Protestant country. All that cerebral debate about the meaning of life and the intellectual feuds French philosophers seem to delight in could have found an outlet in Protestantism, notoriously prone to splits and estrangements over points of theory.

46. A Politician Must Lay Down the Lives of Others to Succeed

At the start of the French Wars of Religion in 1562 Catherine de Medici, from a powerful Italian family, was regent of France. She was a consummate politician – Niccolò Machiavelli's handbook of cynically practical government, *The Prince,* was dedicated to her father, and Catherine had learned its lessons well. Although the great-niece of Pope Leo X, she recognised that persecuting Protestants didn't work. Ten years on in 1572, she was patiently stitching together a political solution between the two religious groups, as well as astutely steering a course that would maintain her position at the top of the heap in the factions of the French court. There the ultra-Catholic Guise family were her sworn enemies; Protestants were just political opponents. In an attempt to see both adversaries off, she used or maybe instigated the Massacre of St Bartholomew's Eve on the night of 23/24 August 1572. For diplomatic reasons, on 18 August her daughter Marguerite had been married to Henri III of Navarre, the Protestant ruler of a state on the border with Spain. Everyone who was anyone was assembled in Paris to celebrate the nuptials. When an attempted assassination of the Huguenot leader Admiral Coligny failed on 22 August Catherine was quick to blame the Guises, who may have been responsible, although she herself might have seen this as an opportunity to pick off a leading Huguenot and blame her enemies.

Goading Catherine's young son King Charles IX into a state of paranoia about Protestant reprisals for the assassination was not difficult. Who actually did this is not resolved, but an order was issued to kill the Huguenot nobles in Paris. Wounded Coligny was dragged from his bed and murdered. Marguerite was actually with her mother when the massacre started but was ignorant of it. Her sister, who was in on the scheme, told her not to join her husband, but Catherine ordered her to go. Marguerite rejoined Henri. When assassins broke in she pleaded for his life. Either this or his promise to convert to Catholicism did the trick and he was allowed to escape.

Despite the king's orders to cease, the massacre spread to the provinces and an estimated 10,000 Protestants died. Although it was initially greeted with joy in some quarters – Philip of Spain is said to have laughed for the only time in his life when he heard the news, and the Pope issued a commemorative medal – it soon became clear this had simply renewed more violent hostilities between the two religious factions. The slaughter was condemned across Europe, even by other Catholic rulers and eventually by the Pope himself. The attempt to sacrifice her own daughter Marguerite, which would both have allowed Catherine to deny involvement as well as ensuring the success of her plans, was not Catherine's only failure: the massacre itself became the major political blunder of her rule.

47. THE HOME OF DRACULA BECAME THE MOST ECUMENICAL EUROPEAN COUNTRY

Bram Stoker's fictional Count Dracula was based on a genuine medieval king of Transylvania, today a province of Romania but until 1526 a principality under Hungarian rule. Vlad III Drāculea (1431–76/7, or maybe not yet dead) was known as 'the Impaler' for his preferred method of executing enemies: driving a spike through them and leaving them in a public place to die. His homeland is therefore an unlikely place to find a culture of religious toleration.

On the border between Asia and Europe, Hungary has been a trading crossroads for centuries, so it has always had a cosmopolitan population. At the time of the Reformation, like much of central Europe, it came under the overlordship of the Catholic Holy Roman Empire, but to the south in the Balkans and Greece Orthodoxy was the predominant faith, while to the north were countries with ties to Russian Orthodoxy. To the east was the Islamic empire of Suleiman the Magnificent, who got an itch to expand his territories. At the Battle of Mohacs in 1526 he defeated and killed Hungary's king. Suleiman was not powerful enough to occupy the whole country and its dependencies, so it was portioned out between the Ottoman Empire in the centre, the Habsburgs in the west and the Principality of Transylvania in the east, which became independent.

In the Turkish-ruled sector Christians of whatever kind were second-class citizens, but did have freedom of worship. The Turks were too busy defending their conquests to involve themselves with their vassals' theological nitpicking. The Hungarians in the west turned to Protestantism, finding its militant message of battling the forces of corruption resonated with them against their Catholic rulers.

In 1558 in Transylvania, both Catholics and Lutherans were declared equally free to practise their religion, although Calvinism was banned, toleration only going so far. Ten years later this freedom was extended to all faiths and persecution on religious grounds was outlawed. Elsewhere in Europe religious wars were being fought, martyrs were being created on both sides and all religious affiliations were fighting each other, often to the death. In 1583 the government went one step further, making the three religions official and adding a fourth, Unitarianism, to the list. The Orthodox Christian Church was also granted toleration.

This astonishing co-existence could not last in the atmosphere of the day. It ended with the Thirty Years War in 1616, when Hungary was drawn in on the Habsburg side while Transylvania opted for the Protestants. At the end of the war in 1648 the Habsburg emperor imposed his religion on Hungary. Noblemen converted on pain of losing their lands and power, the Jesuits' excellent schools spread the Catholic word and Protestant pastors were exiled, sent to work camps or to row as galley slaves. This repression brought a backlash and in 1681 a degree of toleration was accorded to Protestants, but this was a long way from the unique but brief interlude of ecumenicalism enjoyed in Transylvania at the height of the Reformation.

48. MI5 Had Its Origins in Elizabethan England

One of the definitions of a diplomat is 'a man sent abroad to spy for his country'. As long as there have been international relations, ambassadors have been bribing servants and the disaffected to get information on the great and the not-so-good to send back to their masters. Businessmen and soldiers were also paid to keep their eyes open and report back. Everyone knew they were doing it and, as long as they didn't overstep gentlemanly limits, it was tolerated. But the Reformation introduced a new element. There had always been rebels against monarchs and governments, but now those who wanted to replace it were on a religious crusade – the jihadists of their day. Instead of sending spies overseas, the government needed to set up a network to uncover the enemies within: not those who were openly campaigning for change, but who were outwardly conforming while secretly planning for a change of regime.

Elizabeth I's long reign saw various plots against her, mainly on behalf of Mary, Queen of Scots. Francis Walsingham, Secretary of State, is often referred to as her spymaster. He was a convinced Protestant, using his own money to pursue Catholic plotters in England with personal commitment and torture. He worked closely with William Cecil, Elizabeth's chief advisor. Cecil took over as Secretary of State when Walsingham died in 1590, and then in 1598 Cecil's son, Robert, who learned the arts of duplicity and espionage at his father's knee, took over the job. Robert Cecil was responsible for the foiling of the Gunpowder Plot against James I in 1605. The outrage this plot unleashed meant Catholics got the message – no secret plot to assassinate the king was going to work – but the spymasters didn't know this. Following the Glorious Revolution and the installation of the Protestant William of Orange on the English throne, the exiled Stuarts' failed attempts to regain the crown were hardly secret, but closet supporters needed to be kept under surveillance. After the British victory in the Seven Years War (1754–63), espionage became mainly focused overseas on the defeated states' plans for a return match, but fears of treason at home never fully faded. From now on, internal sedition would be increasingly on political rather than religious grounds.

In the nineteenth century Irish Fenians, precursors of Sinn Fein, became the chief enemy within. Along with anarchists (mainly Russian) and other malcontents, they kept internal security spies in a job and bureaucrats busy filing reports.

Until 1909 each government department did its own spying. The Secret Service Bureau brought them all together with two sections: the Security Service (MI5) and the Secret Intelligence Service (MI6). MI5 became the best known because its remit is internal security – all the other departments that developed from MI6 are busy gathering the lowdown on other countries. Today religious terrorists are at the top of MI5's list, just as they were under Elizabeth I. From the seventeenth century to the twenty-first, the aims and methods of both plotters and counter-insurgents have a depressing similarity.

49. SCOTLAND WAS SECOND PRIZE FOR JOHN KNOX

Fuming in exile, the Scottish preacher John Knox (*c.* 1513–72) thought his plight was all the fault of women. Everywhere he looked, they were running the show. In his native Scotland the Frenchwoman Mary of Guise was regent, ruling on behalf of her daughter, another Mary. Knox had been enslaved by her compatriots while hiding from her. After two years in the galleys, he escaped to England in 1549, where he was highly respected and became a chaplain to Edward VI. Then Mary I's accession to the throne caused him to flee to mainland Europe in 1554. In France, Catherine de Medici, a distant cousin of the Pope, was regent for her son. He vented his anger in *The First Blast of the Trumpet Against the Monstruous* [sic] *Regiment of Women*, published anonymously in 1558 in Geneva.

Knox didn't mean that the women formed a military squad: regiment meant 'rule' and monstrous meant 'unnatural'. His Biblical studies convinced him that God thought female sovereigns were abnormal, especially Catholic ones called Mary (Catherine isn't mentioned, probably because Knox was living in Dieppe when he wrote the pamphlet). He also maintained it was wrong that women should have any kind of authority over men. His first publication was predictably very popular with reformers and when the Lords of the Congregation, a political anti-Catholic group, took power in Scotland in 1559 they invited Knox to return. In the meantime, his authorship leaked out and a few months after publication Protestant Elizabeth I succeeded Mary I. Elizabeth read his diatribe and took it personally. She was highly offended by Knox's attack and banned his work. She also refused Knox permission to travel back to Scotland through England.

All fired up with Calvinist zeal, Knox returned, determined to create the kind of theocracy he had learned in Geneva and to extend it to England – by far the bigger prize in those days when Scotland was a backwater. Knox regarded himself as 'an Englishman by adoption'. But he had blotted his copybook with Elizabeth: there was no chance she was going to forgive someone who cast doubt on the legitimacy of her rule – she had enough people doing that already. Knox remained in Scotland, where he was powerful, but it was not the glittering prize he wanted for himself.

In 1559 Knox sent a letter to Elizabeth's secretary William Cecil. He would not back down. Instead, like any politician, he said he'd been taken out of context, regretted that the queen found him 'odious' and said he never intended to offend her. Cecil probably saw no reason to pass it on – Elizabeth was capable of serious hissy fits and knew equivocation when she read it. Knox was well – regarded among the strong fundamentalist faction in England and, had he been more diplomatic, might have succeeded in tipping the balance against the lukewarm Protestantism of the Church of England to the full-blooded Presbyterianism that was his legacy in Scotland.

50. Mary, Queen of Scots Was Politically Astute but Emotionally Stupid

Mary, Queen of Scots holds the record for the most married queen in the United Kingdom. While in no way emulating Henry VIII's unhappy record – divorced, beheaded, died, divorced, beheaded, survived – her three husbands all met unpleasant ends.

Born in 1542, Mary became queen at just a few days old upon the death of her father, James V of Scotland. It was determined that the infant queen would be married to the Dauphin of France to cement the Auld Alliance between Scotland and France against their joint enemy, England. At the age of five she was sent to France. She and François married in 1558 and in 1559 he ascended the French throne. But the sickly youth did not occupy it long. An abscess saw him off and in 1560 the widowed Mary returned to Scotland. While she was away many of the ruling class had fallen under the influence of Calvinism. John Knox publicly condemned her not only for her Catholic religion but also for dancing and dressing ornately. Mary was naturally peeved by this discourtesy but acted cannily. She selected most of her council from Protestants and she flattered them by sitting quietly in a corner doing embroidery, as a dutiful Presbyterian woman should, while they got on with running the country.

Many candidates for this desirable widow's hand were proposed but her own choice was her Catholic cousin Henry Stuart, Lord Darnley. After sickly François he looked both an attractive and a safe bet. She was wrong – Darnley turned out to be bent on getting the throne for himself and was prepared to plot with Protestants to achieve his aims. He was also pathologically jealous. After he had her Italian secretary David Rizzio murdered in front of her while she was pregnant, she decided this marriage had no future. Then Darnley fell out with the Protestants and the couple seemed to be reconciled. Mary may have been lulling him into a false sense of security. Whether she actively participated in planning the explosion that killed him or whether the Earl of Bothwell acted on his own initiative is still fertile ground for historians' debates. Whatever her involvement, Bothwell then had her kidnapped – perhaps with her own consent - and probably raped her. Nevertheless, she married him. This was an error on political grounds. Catholics did not recognise Bothwell's divorce nor the couple's Protestant marriage. Protestants did not like Bothwell's arrogance and Mary soon agreed with them, but she still stood by him when a group of peers rose in rebellion. Her loyalty to a man she was beginning to regret marrying cost her the throne. She fled to England and Bothwell escaped to Denmark, where he was imprisoned and died insane.

Mary had no choice about her first marriage but in her second and third she was less than sensible. Her political savvy, which might have let her keep her religion and steer a course through the violently sectarian politics of sixteenth-century Scotland, completely deserted her when in love.

51. The Spanish Armada Failed Because Philip II Could Not Delegate

Philip II of Spain really, really wanted to end Protestantism in England – and to stop the pesky English supporting their Dutch co-religionists rebelling against him in the Spanish Netherlands. When he decided to launch his Armada in 1588 the odds looked favourable. The Spanish fleet was smaller than the English one, but it was composed of larger, more powerful vessels and had 50 per cent more guns.

The admiral he selected, the Duke of Medina-Sidonia, was a soldier who had never been to sea before and suffered from seasickness. Instead of leaving him to make decisions in response to events on the ground, Philip set out detailed plans in advance and gave orders from some 1,500 km away. Today, it takes more than fourteen hours to drive this distance, but back then a messenger took several days. Philip's strategy was for the Armada to protect the Duke of Parma's army while it was ferried across the Channel in barges from the Netherlands to invade England from Kent. Parma advised against this but Philip took no notice.

On the Armada's way up the Channel, Francis Drake captured one of their ships. He realised that the heavier guns of the Spanish prevented them from being quickly deployed. With this knowledge the English changed tactics, closing in on the Spanish and deliberately firing at their guns to wreck the ships rather than, as was usual then, boarding and killing the crew in hand-to-hand combat.

It dawned too late on the Spanish that the sea off the Netherlands was too shallow to accommodate their ships, so they had to anchor near Calais to wait for the army to march to them. While they were waiting, the English prepared fireships – vessels packed with combustible material, which were set alight and launched on the current towards the Spanish fleet. Although no ships were damaged, they had to scatter to avoid the inferno, and this was the end of their enterprise.

Intermittent encounters continued and by September the Armada was in trouble. Philip had not researched the currents and hazards around Britain, in particular the Gulf Stream, and that caused them huge problems. To escape, the Armada decided to sail round Scotland and Ireland to the Atlantic. This had not been anticipated so food was in short supply. The ships were harried by the English, the Gulf Stream created problems and an exceptionally cold and windy summer – even by Scottish standards – wrecked many ships. The Spanish hoped for help from the Catholics in Ireland, but they were repulsed. Only sixty-seven of 130 ships limped home.

It is simplistic to say that the Spanish Armada failed because Philip II was a control-freak, but opportunities to crush the enemy were missed because they were forbidden by Philip or not anticipated by him, and his underlings dared not disobey. The ill-advised decisions he made and his failure to have a Plan B in the event of bad weather (always foreseeable in Britain) were the major factors. None of this, however, convinced him that God was not on his side.

52. Puritans Were a Bigger Threat to Elizabeth I than Catholics

There were four major plots against Elizabeth I masterminded by Catholics: the Rising of the North (1569), the Ridolfi Plot (1571), the Throgmorton Plot (1583), and the Babington Plot (1586). All aimed to have Elizabeth assassinated and replaced by Mary, Queen of Scots. They were well-organised plans, with foreign support and presumably with papal approval. Such was the spy system run by Francis Walsingham, however, that they had little chance of success. Because so many people were involved, they were open to infiltration. The few obsessive nutters who made attempts on the queen's life on their own initiative were probably more dangerous, as such loners rarely appear on official radars. The motives of an MP, William Parry, who planned to kill the queen but was so awed by her presence he could not carry out his design, have never been determined. Although he might have been a pro-Catholic double agent, he may have been a Puritan.

Extreme Protestants, called Puritans because they wanted to purify the Church of all Catholic elements, were arguably more of a threat. Elizabeth I's middle-of-the road policy did not go far enough for them. They were dangerous because many occupied influential posts as dissident clergymen, civic authorities and even MPs. Following the 1559 Act of Uniformity these reformers waged war on the Anglican Church. They fought a guerrilla war, not with armed men but with tedious books and pamphlets, mainly violent, nagging criticisms of people and practices, countered by lengthy, defensive replies from members of the establishment.

These theological spats probably alienated more people than they convinced and the majority of the population regarded the tedious theological battles with profound apathy.

In 1588, the year of the Spanish Armada, a new and more dangerous Puritan player appeared. Previous writings were verbose and tedious, but this wordsmith was *funny*. Ridicule is more dangerous than po-faced solemnity. He called himself Martin Marprelate (i.e. Damagebishop). After being raided in London, he and his printer travelled into the country, hauling around a bulky press and heavy type, where sympathisers sheltered them. Marprelate issued a series of witty attacks on the weaknesses of the Church of England. Serious effort, including torturing possible informants, went into trying to discover and silence this saucy symptom of a widespread threat to the established Church, but his identity has never been established. Some twenty-two possible candidates have been proposed, but the most likely is Job Throckmorton, an MP for Northampton, one of a large and religiously divided clan, and related to the Catholic Francis Throgmorton whose pro-Catholic plot had been defeated. Marprelate gave people something interesting to read.

The Puritan reformers never reached the critical mass needed, nor did they understand how to engage the man in the Elizabethan street, but they were more dangerous in the long run to the Elizabethan settlement because they were insiders. They occupied influential positions in government, both national and local, and socially as landowners and employers, unlike the Catholic plotters, who were outsiders excluded from power.

53. WITHOUT THE REFORMATION THE WELSH LANGUAGE WOULD HAVE DIED

At the time of the Reformation, Wales was an isolated rural society where the majority of the poorer inhabitants spoke Welsh. The local priests were badly paid, badly educated and largely ignorant of or else ignored Catholic teachings (many, for example, were married). They were rarely visited by their English-speaking bishops and superiors. The country and its language were not high on anyone's list of priorities and religious houses were already in decline. When the Act of Supremacy and the Dissolution of the Monasteries arrived there was very little overt opposition. Most of the clergy signed the Oath of Supremacy with no protests. Only 250 or so monks, nuns and friars were actually displaced and they went quietly. The landowners, on whom the majority of the population depended for their livings, acquiesced with the changes, from which many benefited.

The Reformation brought a requirement to hold services in the local language. Although there was a long tradition of lawmaking, poetry and storytelling in Welsh, it was an oral culture and there were no publications. The first printed book in Welsh, *Yn y Lhyvyr Hwnn* (*In this book ...*), containing the Creed, the Lord's Prayer and the Ten Commandments, was published in 1546 by Sir John Price of Brecon, scholar and Secretary of the Council of Wales and the Marches. It was followed by translations of various religious texts, including a New Testament. The English rulers, however, remained committed to stamp out what they saw as a primitive language spoken by peasants and required English bibles in the churches.

Mary I's reign (1553–58) produced a brief interruption. For the most part the Welsh went back to Roman Catholicism as easily as they had renounced it, suggesting either the old beliefs had a stronger hold than had appeared or it made very little difference to the average person who did not really understand the theological arguments. After Elizabeth I ascended the throne, the need for a Welsh Book of Common Prayer, which appeared with a New Testament in 1567, was successfully argued, and finally in 1588 a complete text of the Bible, translated into elegant Welsh, appeared. This preserved the more literary form of the language and prevented it surviving only as a collection of regional, colloquial dialects, but it was actually a Catholic, Gruffudd Robert, who published the first Welsh grammar in 1567 while in exile for his faith.

Under Elizabeth I more Welshmen were appointed to High Church office in the principality and they took the Welsh language seriously, publishing other grammars and dictionaries. Catholic practices, however, were not easily dislodged: the Welsh may have only superficially acceded to the religious changes imposed on them for the sake of a quiet life. In the 1590s Elizabeth's beady eye was turned on them. Priests were rooted out and pilgrimages to shrines banned. Eventually, however, the translation of the Bible and other religious works, like spiritual diaries, entrenched Protestantism in Wales and preserved the language, although that was far from the original intention.

54. SPAIN'S ECONOMIC DECLINE WAS THE RESULT OF BANKROLLING CATHOLICISM

The self-appointed defender of Catholicism around the world, Philip II of Spain (1527–98), was the son of Charles V, the Holy Roman Emperor, who made him ruler of Spain, the Low Countries, Burgundy and Sicily in 1555. Philip's unsuccessful attempts to suppress heresy abroad impoverished his country, leading to a catastrophic economic decline.

France was particularly wary of Spain's clout and in 1556, shortly after Philip's accession, joined with the Pope, aiming to expel foreign powers from Italy, so Philip found himself at war with Pope Paul IV. Throughout his reign he saw himself as more Catholic than the Pope, who was only obeyed when it was in Spain's interests. At the same time, the Low Countries were trying to throw off Catholic rule. Over twelve years Philip poured mind-boggling sums of money into this theatre of war, but at his death had only partially succeeded. He kept the southern Low Countries in the Catholic fold, but by 1606 the northern provinces, today's Netherlands, had won independence and Protestantism.

Internally Philip needed to keep the Moriscos (Muslims nominally converted to Catholicism) and Marranos (Jews nominally converted to Catholicism) from rebelling, as the Moriscos actually did in 1567 with support from Spanish Protestants. Philip also faced threats from the North African Muslim states, only a few miles across the Mediterranean. These threats necessitated armed forces. His brother defeated the Turkish navy, which had support from the French, in a 1571 sea battle. This produced a little breathing space, but Philip hardly had time to draw breath before deciding to invade his neighbours. The Portuguese showed no sign of wanting to become Protestant, but Philip overpowered them anyway in 1580. Next on his list of countries to reclaim for Catholicism was England. The expensive Spanish Armada, the largest fleet ever assembled for a single engagement, was wrecked and scattered, marking the end of Spain as a naval power. A year later, when Protestant Henry of Navarre became heir to the French throne, Philip channelled money and men to help the Guise family, sworn enemies of reform, but in vain.

Although silver poured in from the extensive Spanish Empire in the Americas and the colonies of the Far East, troops were needed to defend it and missionaries were needed to convert the natives, and it was never enough to cover what Philip spent. It wasn't just his mainly unsuccessful foreign military ventures and successful suppressions of internal unrest that impoverished the state. Running the Inquisition and many religious establishments at home and abroad were a financial drain. He regarded them as necessary to the maintenance and spread of Catholicism, but they produced very little economic benefit to the state. He was forced to borrow money at exorbitant rates. He also forbade Spaniards to study at foreign universities, which cut them off from intellectual and technical developments in Europe. At his death, he left debts that could not be repaid, and a decline in the supply of silver from the Empire, which peaked in the late sixteenth century, finished any hope of a rapid recovery.

55. Keeping the Reformation Out of Portugal Led to Its Decline As Well

Thanks to its venturesome explorers, at the beginning of the fifteenth century Portugal was one of the richest countries in Europe and growing in political importance, largely because of its colonial conquests in South America. It was one of the first nations to trade with Africa, both in slaves and more respectable goods like gold, and also with Japan. All of the European powers became prosperous from similar foundations, but Portugal, though one of the trailblazers, failed to capitalise because it spent too much on fighting the Reformers.

In 1536 the Inquisition was introduced. Initially it was mainly directed against Jews, who were as important in commerce and business in Portugal as they were in other countries. Those who were not executed (an estimated 40,000) quickly fled abroad, so a large tranche of wealth-creators were lost. The Inquisition did not produce anything, it simply consumed time and money suppressing people's thoughts (a lesson all totalitarian states with secret police forces seem unable to learn) and created a climate of fear in which people were unwilling to trust others. Business depends on a degree of trust.

Then, for a crucial period in the Reformation between 1580 and 1640, Portugal became a Spanish province under the control of Philips II, III and IV. Spain was spending a disproportionate amount of its revenue on fighting the Protestant Dutch and British and the Muslim Ottomans in order to extend Catholicism. The wars it was fighting with Catholic France were for political not religious reasons, but still cost money.

To fund all this, Spain happily plundered Portugal's resources.

The Inquisition in Portugal was beefed up to Spanish standards with concomitant expenses. No doubt witnessing heretics being burned alive was a timely warning to other Catholics who might consider letting an unorthodox thought pass through their minds. Maybe an idea about how to improve their business could turn out to be heretical. The sugar plantations in Brazil, initially a Portuguese colony, were taken over by the Dutch between 1630 and 1654. When the Portuguese regained them, they reintroduced the Inquisition, causing many Jewish plantation owners to flee. More crucially, these refugees took the techniques of sugar production to the colonies in the Caribbean owned by the British, Dutch and French. Competition flourished to the detriment of the Portuguese economy.

Although the Inquisition was the primary reason for Portugal's economic decline and consequent loss of influence in Europe, there were other factors. To regain its independence, Portugal decided to fight a twenty-year war against Spain, further depleting its wealth. While this was going on the British, Dutch and French moved in on the overseas markets where Portugal had enjoyed a monopoly. Then in 1755, a gigantic earthquake devastated the capital, Lisbon. Though this was long after the Reformation it really set the seal on the country's attempts to re-establish itself. Some people interpreted this as God's judgment, others concluded that there was no God. Whatever the reason, Portugal never recovered its previous eminence on the world stage.

56. Reform Introduced Democracy

In most early societies the person who rose to the top and gained ultimate power was considered to have succeeded through the approval of a deity. He, or very occasionally she, might be considered divine before or after death. Naturally this was a doctrine that appealed to rulers and in Christianity it was called the divine right of kings. The monarch was, in theory, answerable only to God and had absolute authority in political and religious issues. In practise, any sovereigns who did not temper their whims to the prevailing power struggles of the day risked being despatched to answer to God rather sooner than they anticipated.

Catholicism endorsed this doctrine with the proviso that the monarch needed to obey God's law, i.e. do what he was told by the Church. Fundamental Protestants also believed that, since everything was ordained by God as part of his plan, rulers needed to have his divine approval as determined by pastors. The Reformation brought more and more previously unquestioned beliefs under scrutiny and theologians of all faiths began to look for circumstances in which tyrants could be removed. It would be the people who decided whether or not God approved of a particular sovereign.

Protestant James VI of Scotland and I of England (reigned 1603–25) and over the Channel Catholic Louis XIV of France (1643–1715) were particularly keen on the divine right of kings. Both James's son, Charles I, and Louis's great-grandson Louis XVI lost their heads, literally, because of their failure to adjust to changed realities.

57. THE WORLD'S BESTSELLING BOOK WAS WRITTEN BY A COMMITTEE

In general the need for committees to compromise goes against the production of anything outstanding. As the old joke has it, a camel is a horse designed by a committee. Yet the Authorised Version of the Bible, known in the USA as the King James Version, was actually produced by six committees and has sold more copies than any other book since its first publication in 1611.

Even before the Reformation took hold in England there had been translations of some parts of the Bible into English, which were copied by hand and passed from person to person, like *samizdat* literature in the Soviet bloc of the twentieth century. Then William Tyndale took it upon himself to produce a published translation. But he was no reformer: he was ordained as a Roman Catholic priest in 1521 when he was twenty-seven. Long before that he had begun his task. Tyndale learned Latin, Greek, Hebrew, French, Spanish and Italian and in 1525 published his translation of the New Testament. Because of opposition in England (where Henry VIII was still an obedient Catholic) it had to be printed in Cologne, where Tyndale was then living. The king attempted to seize all 6,000 copies of this Bible to suppress it, but failed. Tyndale had to flee to the Low Countries and went into hiding in Antwerp, which was then under the rule of the devoutly Catholic Spanish Habsburgs. Betrayed by an Englishman, he was burned at the stake in 1536.

By now the reformers had decided that the Bible should be accessible to all, which meant in their own language. Miles Coverdale, an Englishman, had worked with Tyndale and a few years later produced a version of Tyndale's original. He was either luckier or just more canny in his timing. By 1539 Henry VIII had broken with Rome and he authorised this version, called the Great Bible, to be used in churches. When James I of England (James VI of Scotland) came to the throne in 1603 there were a number of other translations and versions in use. James, who rightly prided himself on being a Biblical scholar, thought this undesirable. He recruited fifty-four respected scholars with a wide range of linguistic skills and divided them into six committees. Sections of the Bible were divided between them, depending on their areas of expertise. After they had finished their work, two men from each committee came together to combine the six committees' work into a coherent whole. Finally, the General Committee of Revision met in 1609 to examine the end result. About 80 per cent of Tyndale's original translation survived into the final version. With some minor revisions, this new version was presented to the king, who approved. In 1611 it was launched on the world market. It was not cheap. A bound copy cost 12s and a loose leaf copy cost 10s – five or six weeks' earnings for a farm labourer. A year later a smaller and cheaper edition came out and believers have never looked back.

58. Remaining Catholic in Stuart England Was Expensive

'Recusant' is derived from Latin meaning 'to refuse'. Those who refused to attend Church of England services from about 1570 to 1791 were known as recusants. The word has come to be applied to Catholics, but there were also Protestants who refused to take part in services they regarded as little better than Catholicism. In mainland Europe, refusal to participate in the rites of whichever happened to be the favoured religion usually meant a swift execution. Although in England some recusants were condemned to death on political grounds, a subtler and more lucrative approach was preferred. Catholics were to be hit in their pockets: forced to choose between their conscience and their purse. Under Elizabeth they could be fined for not attending an Anglican service, needed permission to travel more than five miles from their home and faced confiscation of their property. Initially recusants were fined 12s for non-attendance at church at a time when a craftsman earned about 4s a week. Later it was increased to a massive £20 a month. This was halved to £10 per month for wives. So husbands pitched up at church, while the rest of the family stayed at home. It was undoubtedly galling to know that the fines imposed went to support the government that oppressed them.

In the wake of the Gunpowder Plot a draconian piece of legislation was introduced in 1606. Anyone who wanted any kind of government post had to swear an oath of allegiance to the English monarch and to deny the authority of the Pope. No good Catholic felt able to disrespect his spiritual leader in this way. Depriving people of lucrative jobs was swiftly followed by a tax double whammy. In 1625 Catholics had to pay twice as much tax as everyone else. The requirement to attend the Church of England was beefed up as well. If they wanted an official post they needed to take Holy Communion in an Anglican service. Further pieces of legislation were passed. Finally, the opposite tack was tried: toleration. In 1672 the penal laws against Catholics were softened. There was an immediate outcry and the next year the oath and taking Anglican Communion was reimposed on those who wanted an official post. A succession of acts were passed discriminating against Catholics, until finally in 1791 all penalties – economic, social, fiscal – were removed, except for one. Any member of the royal family who wanted to become or marry a Catholic would not be allowed to succeed to the throne – but at least they wouldn't be fined.

Some well-to-do families managed to keep their heads above water and have remained Catholic to the present day, even if it has meant losing power and money. Others decided that a good job to support their family was more important. Either way, the government was able to maintain that it did not kill people for following their consciences, unlike all those unsubtle foreigners on the Continent.

59. THE GUNPOWDER PLOT AND ITS FAILURE WAS A FAMILY AFFAIR

Today the only name most people associate with the Gunpowder Plot of 1605 is Guy Fawkes, but along with him were a group of interrelated Catholics who hoped to blow up the House of Lords, killing King James I and most, if not all, of the MPs at the state opening of Parliament on 5 November. The plan was to replace them with Catholics who would restore the old faith to England. Scotland would have to come later, as it was still a separate nation and the Presbyterians there would be harder nuts to crack. James's wife, Anne of Denmark, was a convert to Catholicism, so it was planned to put the couple's eldest son on the throne with her, suitably advised, as regent.

Robert and Thomas Wintour were brothers, John Grant was their brother-in-law, Robert Catesby their cousin and Francis Tresham their first cousin once removed. Jack and Christopher Wright were brothers and Thomas Percy was their brother-in-law. Robert Keyes and Ambrose Rookwood were cousins by marriage. All the families were among the Catholic gentry who were connected by marriage to members of the nobility. Robert Catesby was the driving force. They recruited an unrelated soldier, Guy Fawkes, who had been at school with the Wright brothers, for his knowledge of explosives. Security was somewhat lax in those days. The conspirators took a lease on a cellar within the Palace of Westminster, actually underneath the House of Lords. Over a few months the plotters brought barrels of gunpowder into the cellar and by November they were ready to light the touchpaper and retire to safety.

The betrayal of their plot might also have been a family affair. A letter was delivered to Francis Tresham's brother-in-law, Lord Monteagle, warning him not to attend the opening of Parliament. Who wrote the letter has still not been determined – suspects include Monteagle himself – but the result was the unravelling of the plot. The cellars beneath the House of Parliament were searched and Guy Fawkes, along with thirty-six barrels of gunpowder, was found and arrested. The other plotters fled, but under torture Fawkes disclosed the whole plan and those who made it.

The authorities pursued the fugitives. None escaped. Catesby and Grant were hurt when the group tried to dry gunpowder and it exploded. Later, Catesby and Percy were shot. The survivors were all rounded up and threatened with torture. Whether this was carried out or not is unknown, but they talked. Along with the conspirators some Catholic priests were implicated and one was executed. All the conspirators, and two brothers who had sheltered them, were hanged, some with the additional punishment of being drawn and quartered – that is cut down while still alive, castrated and cut into pieces.

For centuries, the thwarting of the Gunpowder Plot was officially celebrated. Now it is just an excuse for a party and the role of all the related plotters has all but been forgotten. Only Guy Fawkes is remembered.

60. Oppression Improved the Dutch Economy

At the time of the Reformation the Low Countries, an area of Northern Europe covering today's Netherlands, Luxembourg and parts of northern France, belonged to the Holy Roman Empire. Trading links with Germany and Switzerland brought reformed ideas, which really caught on. When the Emperor Charles V abdicated in 1555 the region was inherited by his son, Philip II of Spain. Charles had been – by the standards of the day – relatively liberal. Although the Inquisition was introduced in 1522 and the first Protestant martyr was burned at the stake a year later, persecutions were initially intermittent. In 1562 Philip sent in the Duke of Alva to crack down on Protestants and the severities he introduced triggered first a wave of migrants and then, in 1566, outright rebellion against Spanish rule.

The seventeen provinces in this area were often at loggerheads, but in 1579 nine of them decided they hated the Spanish more than they hated each other, and these United Provinces of the Netherlands came together in a republic led by William of Orange, a Catholic. The southern provinces accepted Spanish rule, but a state of war between Spain and the northern United Provinces erratically continued until 1648. By 1606, however, the Dutch Republic had established enough independence to go its own heretical way. Initially Lutheran, the Dutch later embraced Calvinism, but were too busy making money to maintain their independence to persecute anyone who was contributing to their prosperity. Numerous Protestant sects, including the generally despised Anabaptists, found a degree of toleration, and there was also a large Jewish community. Even

Catholics were allowed to live here, as long as they didn't do anything to reveal their faith in public.

Despite being a tiny country and heavily taxed to fight the might of the Spanish Empire, by the end of the hostilities the Dutch Republic had the most flourishing economy in Europe. Its extensive, government-owned trading links with Africa and East Asia brought great riches. The lack of land led to the creation of an urban society. Most European countries at this time were predominantly agricultural – they had a lot of land and peasants to work it. The Republic had towns and didn't want quite so many peasants; it needed skilled artisans. Amsterdam became a centre for diamond cutting. The profits from that and other businesses created a banking industry. The geographical disadvantages created by its low-lying land led to the development of engineering skills that could be exported to other places, like the English Fens. Refugees from repression in the southern, Spanish-ruled provinces also boosted its skills base. By 1600 Amsterdam had overtaken Antwerp both in population and trade. It was not only Antwerp that suffered commercially. The need to spend so much on fighting to regain the nine provinces inflicted considerable, some might argue irreparable, damage to the Spain's economy. The desire to retain independence from one of the major powers in Europe combined with the disadvantages imposed by nature made the Dutch resourceful.

61. America Was Founded by People Who Couldn't Get On With Their Neighbours

The first permanent English settlement was established by the Virginia Company in 1607 in Jamestown, Virginia. Although the stated aim was to find precious metals and minerals and to trade, a number of the first 100 colonists were gentlemen, not used to work of any kind. Why they chose to travel halfway round the world to labour like peasants is not known, but it must be surmised that either they couldn't hack it at home or their families were glad to see the back of them. At first they dealt well with the Native Americans, but relations soon soured and armed conflict began. It lasted for ten years, until 1632. The next influx of immigrants had a religious motive. Their conflict was with their compatriots.

Around the beginning of the seventeenth century some separatists in Eastern England decided they wanted no contact with those who did not agree with them at home and moved to the Netherlands to join other congregations with similar beliefs. But they couldn't get on with their neighbours there either – they found their children were becoming more Dutch than English - so they set off to North America among the 102 *Mayflower* pilgrims who landed at Plymouth Rock in Massachusetts in 1624. It's no surprise they found it so difficult to settle, for they were formed in the image of their originator, Robert Browne. He started out as an Anglican vicar but formed the first-ever group to secede from the Church of England around 1579 because he didn't agree with the Puritan movement's aim to reform from within. In 1581 he moved to the

Netherlands, but fell out with his co-religionists there: the church they established lasted only two years. In 1585 he returned to the Church of England, becoming a schoolmaster and parish minister back in England. His former followers regarded him as a traitor and two of them engaged in virulent correspondence with him. Words were not his only weapons: he was arrested for hitting his godson and died in a Northampton jail in 1633. These first separatists were followed by all shades of religious belief. Initially they were mainly Protestant, but some Catholics arrived to escape persecution. Other denominations, like Mormonism (the Church of Latter-Day Saints), Adventists, Jehovah's Witnesses and myriad others are indigenous, founded by people who couldn't compromise with what was already on offer.

Whether the founders of America were seeking religious freedom, fighting for liberty, escaping persecution or determined to create a society in which everyone did as God told them to, they were not people who were prepared to compromise for the sake of social harmony. Once in America they had the space to up sticks and move away from anyone with whom they disagreed and set up their own colonies – virtually impossible in densely populated Europe where every inch of land is owned by someone.

62. Witchcraft Increased under Protestantism

A perpetual problem for the church authorities has always been to distinguish between visions and activities that have a divine purpose and those that come from the Devil. In periods of social unrest during medieval times there were intermittent trials for witchcraft in Europe, but it was not until the Reformation that accusing people of compacts with Satan became a continent-wide craze.

The Biblical injunction that 'thou shalt not suffer a witch to live' (Exodus 22:18) was a spur to the Protestants who saw the Bible as the ultimate lifestyle guide. Even kings got in on the act: James VI of Scotland and I of England wrote *Daemonologie* to prove the existence of witches. In times of social uncertainty and change, people look for scapegoats – someone to blame for the misfortunes they see around them – and the Reformation created huge turbulence. But it wasn't just Protestants who saw witches behind every bush. In the German lands at the height of the Thirty Years War, it was two places ruled by prince-bishops, Bamberg and Würzburg, that saw the most ferocious persecutions. It was not that magical practices increased under Protestantism, it was that people felt powerless and wanted to control and stabilise their surroundings. Spain and Italy, resolutely Catholic, saw comparatively few witch-hunts.

Easy targets for blame were the poor and powerless who transgressed social norms, like being unmarried. Almost all the victims of witch-hunts were lower class, marginalised and mainly women, although some men and a few of those from higher up the social scale were targeted. An element of revenge and envy was also present in many accusations. Most of those who admitted to witchcraft did so under torture, both physical and mental, and readily confirmed what their tormentors suggested they had done. These confirmations were used as the basis to question other supposed witches and were undoubtedly embellished by the fantasies of both the accused and the interrogator. The craze crossed the ocean to America, where witches were being discovered among the Protestant migrants long before the Salem witch trials in 1692. The accusers here were successful until they targeted the powerful. It is estimated that some 80,000 individuals were tried and 35,000 executed across Europe and North America. With growing rationalism and the abatement of religious persecution, belief in witchcraft faded and those who actually believed in magic became regarded as deluded rather than dangerous.

However, even today belief in witches is not dead, surviving in Africa, India, Papua New Guinea and in the USA. In the 1980s an entirely unfounded theory of international satanic ritual abuse of children surfaced in the US, predominantly among people with strong Protestant beliefs, which was also uncritically accepted by therapists and social workers in Britain. The methods, now discredited, used by those collecting evidence were remarkably similar to those practised by witchfinders in the past, planting ideas which would surface as recovered memories. Although children suffer sexual abuse, it is no longer credible that this is part of a widespread cult of devil-worship.

63. THE REFORMATION CREATED EUROPEAN COLONIALISM

Colonialism is based on trade. The aim is to bring in money and resources to boost the homeland's economy, which allows the ruling classes to live in the style to which they think they are entitled. Hard on the heels of traders come administrators to impose a bureaucracy modelled on the colonial power's homeland and a military presence to keep the peasantry under control. The subjects can then be called on to pay taxes, fight in wars or just prevent other potential emperors from moving in. The Egyptian Empire, the Roman Empire (on which the British later modelled themselves) and the Chinese Empire, among many others, long pre-date the Reformation. But the Reformation added a novel twist to this pattern: missionaries.

Previous empires were polytheistic and had an elastic attitude to deities: the more the merrier was their motto. Local gods were easily added and worshipped alongside the standard pantheon. Religion was not allowed to interfere with commerce or military might. The Spanish and Portuguese initially created their empires in the Americas with the aim of getting their hands on precious metals to replenish their homelands' coffers, but also realised that the locals would boost the Catholic Church's population. In return for a cut of money and converts, the Pope divided up the world trading rights between these two countries. Soon after the Reformation the Dutch and the English entered the race. Neither considered that the Pope had any authority to decide whether they should be allowed to trade somewhere and they set up outposts in Asia and Africa, as well as the Americas. Not to be outdone, the

French decided they had to join in so they wouldn't be left behind. Their traders were swiftly followed by missionaries of the various strands of faith competing for hearts, minds and souls. The locals who wanted the goodies on offer – education, employment, access to other advantages – realised it paid to fall in line. Finally, the armed forces moved in to establish and maintain the authority and cultural values of the different mother countries.

Although the Reformation did not create European colonialism, it made it more bitterly competitive than previous empires. Christianity is monotheistic, but the various strands produced by the Reformation could not agree on how their sole god should be worshipped. All branches justified themselves by claiming they alone provided the correct road to salvation. The colonial rulers followed them with the high-minded claim they were bringing civilisation to ignorant and primitive peasants.

Between the sixteenth and twentieth centuries, Europe's superior technology made it possible to control and exploit many millions of indigenous peoples. This technology was partly the result of Protestantism – not just the famed work ethic, but also the willingness to think outside the box that their freedom of conscience brought. Although the twentieth century largely brought independence to most of the colonies, the effects of the religious wars in Europe produced by the Reformation continue to reverberate today, particularly in Africa, but increasingly in other ex-colonial lands.

64. The English Civil War Was Britain's War of Religion

From 1639 to 1651 the English were at war with each other and involved in conflicts in Scotland, Wales and Ireland. The whole period of turmoil is described as the War of the Three Kingdoms, in which the English Civil War is just one strand. It was Scotland's resentment of Charles I's attempt to introduce the English Book of Common Prayer to Presbyterians north of the border that lit the fuse. In 1641 the Catholic Irish rose up because they didn't want Anglicanism either.

Charles I was a High Anglican married to a Catholic, Henrietta Maria of France. The smells, bells, pomp and ritual he favoured were, for many, indistinguishable from Roman Catholicism. The Archbishop of Canterbury he appointed in 1633, William Laud, shared his views and planned to impose uniformity of worship. The fear was that the king would be seduced into the arms of Rome – he was more than halfway there already in Puritan eyes. More damagingly, Charles was a firm believer in the divine right of kings. He was convinced he had a hotline to God and was responsible only to him. This clashed with the Parliamentarians' view that the king was answerable to Parliament. The king needed Parliament's consent to raise taxes. MPs saw their power to withhold money as a way of controlling the king. For eleven years from 1629 Charles tried to do without Parliament, raising money by selling jobs and demanding 'contributions' to fund his wars. Briefly, he recalled the MPs in April 1640 to get money to put down the mutinous Scots, then packed them off a month later, but by November his parlous financial state forced him to recall Parliament. The MPs, many of them Puritans like Oliver Cromwell, were seriously disgruntled and they presented a list of complaints. The attempt to impose a more Catholic form of religion was first, but the other three were all about how the king was governing. Tactfully, they said he had been badly advised, but Charles was not going to take this get-out option. After problems getting money to put down the Irish rebellion, in 1642 he tried to arrest five MPs on a charge of treason. This abuse of parliamentary privilege started the English Civil War, but it took a few months of fruitless negotiations for full-scale hostilities to break out. No one wanted a war. As is well known, the king lost the war (and his head) and Oliver Cromwell's Roundheads won.

About 200,000 people perished, but determining who died for political and who died for religious reasons is impossible as they were so closely intertwined. The English Civil War has been called England's War of Religion, but it was primarily a political war at a time when paradigms of rule were inspired by religion. The battle was not between Catholicism and Protestantism, as it was in most of mainland Europe, but between the Anglican and Presbyterian beliefs about how society should be run.

65. THE ENGLISH EXPERIMENT WITH A GODLY REPUBLIC FAILED

Fundamentalist Protestants believed that the state should be run on religious lines, as long as these accorded with their beliefs. After Charles I fatally insisted he was answerable only to God, England experimented with a theocracy – a state ruled on religious grounds – under Oliver Cromwell (1599–1658), who was an unlikely Ayotollah. Cromwell belonged to the minor gentry. By marriage he was connected to a network of Puritan gentry and what role they played in his religious conversion is not known, but at some point, probably in the 1630s, he became an Independent, believing that the Church of England was still too Catholic and needed to be purged. He became an MP in 1628 for his home town of Huntingdon and lived through the roller-coaster ride of Charles I's arbitrary dismissals and summonings of Parliaments, until in 1642 the English Civil War broke out. Cromwell became a leading light as a commander on the victorious Roundhead side. He was one of those who signed the death warrant for Charles I, whose execution in 1649 was followed by the proclamation of a republic. In 1649 and 1650 he commanded a campaign in Ireland which defeated the royalist forces there, and he fought against Scotland in 1650 and 1651. His victories gave him kudos with his fellow MPs who, having deposed the king, were divided on what to do next, and he took command. He saw himself as Moses, bringing his people into the Promised Land, and as having been selected by God.

Despite his earlier experiences with the arbitrary use of power to dispose of Parliaments, Cromwell dismissed Parliament in 1653. His support from the army probably influenced the invitation from his colleagues to become Lord Protector of England, Wales, Scotland and Ireland. Like so many military dictators, he set about imposing a series of repressions. Penal laws were passed against Catholics, especially in Ireland, but they were not the only ones to suffer. In England and Wales theatres were closed and gambling forbidden under Puritan influence. Even celebrating Christmas was been banned as early as 1644. The Commonwealth attempted to impose Puritans in positions of authority to enforce laws; there weren't enough hardliners to go around, so only a few places managed to ban fairs, impose compulsory churchgoing, close alehouses and the like. In addition, people had to listen to endless theological debates and their taxes were increased to maintain the army.

This regime became an awful warning of the fate awaiting those living under godly rule. After seven years of Cromwell, the English had had enough. When he died in 1658, his son Richard failed to win even the army's support. Charles I's son, waiting in the wings in France, might have been a libertine with a string of mistresses, might have been a survivor willing to say and do anything to keep his throne and, horror of horrors, he might have been a suspected Catholic, but he enjoyed life. The English had had enough of no Christmas and no fun, and Charles II was triumphantly restored to the throne in 1660.

66. The Commonwealth Period Saw the Birth of Socialism

The years from the English Civil War to the end of the Commonwealth in 1660 were not just years of religious ferment and experiment. Political theories about the relationship between rulers and the ruled were ignited by reading the Bible. 'When Adam delved and Eve span, who was then the gentleman?' became a popular slogan. If the father and mother of all mankind had worked to maintain themselves, why were all these titled fatcats running the show?

The Levellers were the most influential and best organised of these movements. They wanted government by elected representatives, to extend the suffrage (but only to men, of course), to have common land ownership, equality before the law and religious tolerance. Their leader, John Lilburne, came from a gentry background and, far from being a proto-communist, wanted the abolition of monopolies and to create greater financial and commercial freedom for small capitalists like himself (he was indeed engaged in some very dubious speculations). Their power bases were in the City of London and in the army.

It was not the businessmen that Cromwell took notice of but the army. In 1647 the Levellers conducted the first of three debates in Putney, known prosaically as the Putney Debates. The army representatives had the most influence as they thrashed out the demands they would present to Parliament and they weren't interested in the problems of small capitalism. They saw the Leveller movement in terms of getting their arrears of pay and terms of service sorted. When Cromwell met the leaders to discuss their wishlist he asked just how far they wanted to extend the suffrage. Not actually to servants, apprentices or beggars, came the response. Equality had its limits. Then, to demonstrate the army's power and to prove they were serious, there were mutinies among troopers supporting the Levellers. Alarmed, Cromwell put them down and had many of the leaders executed. He feared that, if the Levellers' propositions were accepted, anarchy would be unloosed.

The Diggers were a much smaller political grouping. Their leader, Gerrard Winstanley, had been a well-to-do freeman of the City of London made bankrupt by the Civil War and reduced to herding cows. He came up with the idea of communal ownership of land and proposed equality law and education between the sexes. The number of his followers was small and divided between four rural sites in England where communities lived on common land, growing their own food, in a forerunner of hippie communes. In 1657 Winstanley's father-in-law gave him some land and he became a pillar of the local parish and community, all ideas of communal ownership of land forgotten. Later still he returned to trade in London.

Karl Marx spent many happy hours in the British Library using the manifestos and pamphlets of these groups – particularly the political ones, which inspired many of his theories and are sometimes claimed as the precursors of socialism. If he had read them more critically, he would have noticed that these two main political movements were created by failed businessmen.

67. The Reformation Improved the Treatment of Jews in Europe

Christianity sees Jesus of Nazareth as the Messiah, the saviour of mankind, and the deity. In the New Testament, it is the Jews who are depicted as responsible for Christ's death. When Pilate asks them what to do, they cry, 'Crucify him.' The refusal to accept Christ as the Messiah, along with their condemnation of him, made Jews figures of hate. Every country had its child saint, like St Hugh of Lincoln, supposedly murdered by Jews to use his blood in their rituals.

They were excluded from positions of power across Europe, usually made to wear a symbol of their faith and often forced to live in ghettos (from the Italian word for 'forge', after the district in Venice to which they were confined). Their status was always insecure. In periods of prosperity they were tolerated for their business activities, like lending money at interest (forbidden to Christians), and their scholarship. In periods of hardship they were useful scapegoats, sometimes simply expelled from a kingdom, but more often massacred, especially when this allowed debts to be wiped out.

Protestant theology drew heavily on the Old Testament, which was regarded by the Catholic Church as of lesser importance. Martin Luther had hoped to convert Jews to his brand of Christianity, but when they refused he demanded the usual violent reprisals against them. Jean Calvin was less ferocious. His views were ambiguous: he accepted that both Jews and Christians were part of the same covenant from God, but was scornful about the Jews he actually met. Reading the Bible, however, gave ordinary Protestants respect for Judaism. They saw the sufferings of many of the people there mirrored in their own experiences of persecution and gave their children names from the Old Testament, rather than the saints favoured by Catholics. Those who fought Catholics called themselves 'Lions of Judah', a Biblical reference from the Old Testament.

Jews had been expelled from England in 1290. Some returned following their expulsion from Spain in 1492, pretending to be converted but in private practising their faith, but they were not officially allowed to live openly in England until 1656, when Oliver Cromwell encouraged a group to come from Amsterdam. His reasons appear to be a combination of financial problems and his fundamentalist belief that the Day of Judgement would not come until Jews lived in every country in the world, as suggested in the Bible. About the same time they began to appear in Scotland. This did not mean that anyone liked them any better and their activities were restricted, but the time of persecution had passed and gradual emancipation began.

The same route was followed in other countries and by the eighteenth century there were Jewish communities in most Protestant states. Although banned from the Papal States, even Catholic countries' attitudes had softened and Jewish communities began to establish themselves, although how far that was due to the reformers' attitudes and influence is a moot point.

68. St Ignatius of Loyola Never Planned to Be a Teacher

Inigo Lopez de Loyola was born in 1491 into a family ennobled for their military exploits in the Basque region of Spain. He is now known as St Ignatius of Loyola. He followed the family tradition and was seriously wounded in battle in 1521. While convalescing, his faith became more intense, and later he studied theology, first in Spain and then in Paris. His arrival here in 1534 coincided with the major anti-Protestant furore that caused Jean Calvin to flee for his life. Inigo was used to military discipline, travelling to hotspots to put down enemies and finding practical solutions to problems. Whether his later actions were inspired by a conviction that with his military training he could have wiped out Calvin and his heretical followers is not recorded.

Ignatius's initial aim was to convert non-Christians in the Holy Land – effectively a crusade – but unable to undertake a pilgrimage to Jerusalem he and ten other priestly pals from Paris decided to go to Rome. Calling themselves the Society of Jesus, in 1539 they offered themselves to the Pope as a kind of private troubleshooting squad, vowing unquestioning obedience. A year later the Pope approved their order. Ignatius was opposed to theological speculation and to the contemplative life (although he developed an influential series of spiritual exercises) and no doubt envisaged his Society taking off to some spot where Protestants were giving grief and taking out their leaders – a sort of spiritual SAS. He assumed his recruits would be mature men, perhaps with a military background, but this active and pugnacious mission soon attracted keen, bright youngsters. Ignatius founded a college to train them to counter Protestant arguments. So good was the teaching that other colleges were established. Well-to-do families clamoured to have their children given a first-rate education without any intention of them entering the Society. Money and influence always win over fine intentions and step-by-step Ignatius's, original aim was diverted into running well-regarded schools and other educational institutions.

Ignatius died in 1556 after thirty-two schools had been established. He had always been a restless man, wanting to be on the move and do things rather than sit and think. But he had taken a vow of unquestioning obedience to the Pope and never left any record of how seriously this was tested as he saw his original plans sidetracked. He did not see the Society of Jesus rapidly become the largest provider of education in Europe. Alumni included many offspring of the princely houses of Europe, which further spread its power and influence. Schools and colleges were also established in the colonies of Catholic countries where their teaching was so respected that local families, whether they had converted to Christianity or not, had their children educated there. In offering an education comparable to the best the Protestants had to offer, the Society of Jesus became one of the most effective movements of the Counter Reformation, but it was far from Ignatius's original, military intention.

69. CATHOLIC WOMEN'S EDUCATION WAS REVOLUTIONISED BY A YORKSHIREWOMAN

Following the Reformation the popes created more religious orders. At first women's orders, like the Company of St Ursula (Ursulines) (1535) and The Order of the Visitation of Holy Mary (1610), worked in the community tending the poor and needy, but this alarming independence meant they were soon put back behind convent walls, regarded as the right place for women. As the Daughters of Charity of St Vincent de Paul (1633) were mainly well-to-do ladies, they were allowed to work from their well-appointed homes.

Education was considered the primary way to ensure immunity against Protestantism. It was the Jesuits, founded as a missionary order but quickly diverted into education, who claimed, 'Give me a child until he is seven and I will give you the man,' but who was actually looking after children up to this age? Women, of course. When it was recognised how important it would be to educate potential mothers to counter Protestantism, from 1595 the Ursulines were switched from looking after the poor to the task of educating girls. In 1639 they became the first nuns to go to the New World when they landed in Canada to teach the native people's children. However, they remained behind convent walls, educating children within their confines.

Englishwoman Mary Ward, born in Yorkshire, believed – shock, horror! – that women were equal to men in intellect and should be educated appropriately. She also believed that women needed to be out in the community and this truly radical idea meant she was lucky not to be condemned as a heretic. In 1609, with a group of strong-minded women, she established a successful girls' school at St Omer in France, modelled on the work the Jesuits were doing with boys. They called themselves the Congregation of Jesus or Institute of the Blessed Virgin Mary, also known as the Loreto Sisters. Mary Ward travelled across Europe, setting up further girls' schools and creating panic in the papacy at the thought of all those women let loose in the community telling girls they were just as clever as boys. Her congregation was suppressed in 1630, but her talent and commitment could not be wasted. In 1639 the Pope of the day sent her to England, where she set up schools in London but did most of her work in her native Yorkshire, where both Catholics and Protestants respected her. Her congregation became two religious orders, but it was not until 1703 that the IBVM was formally recognised. The Congregation of Jesus didn't get the stamp of approval until 1877 and it took until 1909 before Mary Ward's work in founding these two important religious and educational institutes was recognised by the Holy See.

70. Catholics Set Fashions for the Ideal Home of the Seventeenth Century

While Reformers were worshipping in plain chapels, built without ornamentation in a style now called 'Protestant barn' and chanting psalms in a subdued monotone, the Catholic Church decided it needed to communicate religion in a more touchy-feely way. The result was the exuberant, ornamental style known as baroque, which influenced the arts and architecture across Europe from 1600 to about 1725. Both Catholic and Protestant states adopted it, but its most elaborated expression came in Italy, Spain and the Catholic states of Germany. The French favoured a more restrained version and it had little effect in the Low Countries, whose sober middle-class burghers preferred realism and peaceful landscapes. They got their emotional excitement from exotic fruit and flowers depicted in still-life paintings.

Characterised by rich, detailed ornamentation and grandeur, this style is particularly noticeable inside Catholic churches, where all the colours of the rainbow, more textures than a book of carpet samples, plus gilding, plus statues, plus *trompe l'oeil* visual effects, riot over every surface. The ceilings often depict a heaven largely populated by plump cherubs and scantily clad men and women. Walking into such an environment is disorienting – where to look first? What at? It's the artistic equivalent of the military tactic of shock and awe and gave the uneducated something to look at while the Latin service was going on.

Music gave the faithful something to listen to and engaged their emotions. Elaborate settings of masses, interweaving numerous soaring voices, were not confined to Catholic composers like Vivaldi and Monteverdi. Purcell in England and the Lutherans Bach, Handel, Telemann and Schütz also wrote in this fashionable style.

Although initially aimed at keeping the poor and illiterate entertained, the style was enthusiastically adopted by the rich to flaunt their wealth and status. Louis XIV's Versailles set the pattern for rulers who built palaces with an endless succession of dazzling rooms surrounded by high-maintenance formal gardens. The nobility imitated their creations. At the centre of these stately homes was a huge gallery – in Versailles it was lined with expensive mirrors, but usually it was the setting for the owner's art collection. On the walls, on top of textured silk and velvet coverings, hung giant paintings in ornately carved and gilded frames, sometimes depicting religious themes but usually of dramatic events from classical mythology. These too were crowded with individuals, usually in scanty draperies like the inhabitants of heavens in Catholic churches. Such dwellings were designed for public life, to overwhelm one's friends and enemies, but they had their disadvantages: it was virtually impossible to get hot food from the mundane kitchens through a succession of chambers to the formal dining rooms. It was not just this kind of inconvenience that caused baroque to fall out of fashion. Driven by the rationality of the Enlightenment, classicism returned to favour among the fashionistas. By now the Counter-Reformation was over so there was no religious significance behind neoclassicism's less ornate principles, which could be happily adopted by even the most fervent Catholic.

71. Implementing the Council of Trent's Reforms Was Not Easy

The results of the Counter-Reformation can readily be seen in interior decoration (baroque churches and stately homes) and heard in the music produced in the period, but how far the revision of the religious services and practices changed the beliefs and behaviour of the average churchgoer is more difficult to ascertain.

Everywhere the secular authorities were agreed that making the lower orders more obedient to them was a good thing, and this could be achieved by implementing the Council of Trent's reforms and imposing a more moral code of behaviour, including regular attendance at church.

The Jesuits played an active part in modernisation, particularly in urban centres. They created Sodalities of the Blessed Virgin, which aimed to create social commitment to Catholicism among influential lay people according to their social status and occupations. As these provided networking groups for businessmen and artisans they proved very popular. The Jesuits' educational programmes were effective among the ruling classes, but lower down had less effect, where promoting the revised catechism was not very successful, and they had little impact in the countryside. Here traditional monasteries, which were often in conflict with the Jesuits, had more clout.

Although Catholic congregations are often characterised as passive and bovinely obedient to the parish priest, the reality on the ground was rather different, especially in rural areas – always slower to embrace new ways than towns. In south-west Germany particularly, local communes exercised considerable control over the parish priest's appointment and, if he didn't measure up, dismissal. They also controlled local finances, including the spending of tithes in ways that benefited the community. The embedding of Catholicism at a local level was one of the aims of the council, but it meant that the authorities had to learn to live with the jollier aspects of Catholic piety, like pilgrimages, having dances to celebrate marriages and the plethora of holy days that studded the calendar. Nor was it possible to eradicate many of the beliefs and practices that had their origin in pre-Christianity, like reverence paid to water shown in well-dressing and throwing coins into fountains. The reiteration of the veneration of saints and the cult of the Virgin by the Council of Trent had a downside: the uneducated came to regard them as more important than God in their everyday life. In defiance of the church's ordinances, people went on creating their own local saints. In nineteenth-century France the statues of saints who failed to deliver were abused. The emphasis on the Eucharist had the effect of downplaying the importance of the rest of the service and nipping in late, just as the Host was being elevated, remains a practice in many places from Ireland to Italy.

The resolutions of the Council of Trent were formulated by a bunch of academics. Their implementation necessarily involved compromise, but the Catholic Church was good at that and succeeded in a difficult task.

72. Women's Position in Society Was Made Worse by the Reformation

In the Roman Catholic Church, women had opportunities to live relatively independent lives in convents, where they wielded some power and were accorded respect. Young women who did not want to shackle themselves in marriage had a praiseworthy escape route. When widowed, a woman who did not want to remarry could enter a nunnery to live out her days free from the demands of men and children. And, as is well attested, the standards in many women's religious houses did not preclude them from amorous dalliance or other worldly pleasures.

Early Protestantism had no religious houses and women were in theory strictly confined to their own households. There was no escape from a tyrannous husband or father, who, as St Paul said, represented God. St Paul also demanded that women keep silent in church and were not to lecture their husbands or other men. But elsewhere he says there is no male or female in Christ and praises early women followers who instructed others in the new faith. So the men in charge had a choice of model to follow. Unsurprisingly, they chose the more repressive one. In England in 1543 an Act forbade lower-class women to read the Bible and upper-class women were restricted to reading it where no one else could hear them. Many fought back with Biblical justifications and the Act was repealed in 1547.

Women began to gain greater autonomy and influence in the nonconformist denominations. When a breakaway group establishes a new sect, women are usually given better treatment than they receive under the old dispensations. This is partly to recruit more followers and partly to ensure that children are born and brought up in the faith. But it did have a knock-on effect in society when religion was a more important factor than it is today. Women preachers in the Society of Friends (founded in 1647) scandalised contemporary society. Others, like Jane Wardley and Ann Lee of the United Society of Believers in Christ's Second Appearing (the Shakers), themselves became leaders. The Methodists had women deacons from 1890 and began to ordain women in 1974. The national churches followed more slowly. The first Anglican synod to ordain women regularly was that of Hong Kong and Macao in 1971. The others have been falling in ever since, though there remain some, like Nigeria and South East Asia, where women's ministry is still strongly resisted.

The position of women in Roman Catholicism has remained much the same over the centuries. Although the Virgin Mary has an exalted role, she is an impossible ideal. While society outside changed, within the Church the same roles that were available to medieval women applied. New religious orders gave women greater freedom, but they remained limited to the traditional female roles of teaching and nursing. Initially, the Reformation was bad for women's lives and status, but in the long run it helped to improve them.

73. THE REFORMATION PRODUCED THE MODERN NOVEL

Storytelling is as old as language. The Bible is full of rattling good tales. Following the invention of printing in the fifteenth century, prose began to dominate European fiction. It was not only religious works that flowed from the presses: a newly literate readership, swelled by the Protestant desire for individuals to read and understand the Bible, naturally welcomed a bit of light relief from all those turgid theological tomes. The upper classes and middle classes liked poetry and histories, which might be used to criticise current events. Chapbooks recounted legends, told jokes and described miraculous events, but also related true crimes. Although aimed at the cheap end of the popular market, everyone enjoyed them in a *Hello* magazine kind of way.

From these disparate sources, the modern novel, a fictional narrative describing human experiences, usually in prose, emerged in the seventeenth century. Spanish Catholic Miguel de Cervantes is generally regarded as the first novelist. His *Don Quixote* (1605), in which a knight and his servant encounter a series of events, was a satire on medieval romances where gallant heroes meet a series of challenges from fabulous creatures, especially dragons. The French were the first to embrace this new genre. They dropped the dragons but continued to write about aristos and their problems, with which the average peasant could hardly identify. They also used an elaborate, euphemistic lexicon to exclude those outside their circle, which was pretty much everyone.

The new ingredients added by the Reformation were inclusiveness and realism. Though by no means completely democratic in practice, the reformers theoretically considered that everyone was equal before God. Protestants were encouraged not only to read but to write, to keep spiritual diaries, accounts of their daily lives in which they reflected on their religious practice. These included everyday occurrences in which the hand of God was seen. This habit of describing mundane events with significance for everyone, not just a few of the chattering classes, was incorporated into the novel. A Presbyterian tradesman, journalist and political pamphleteer, Daniel Defoe (*c.* 1660–1731) was the first English writer to make ordinary people, like sailors (*Robinson Crusoe*, 1719), soldiers (*Colonel Jack*, 1722) and even prostitutes (*Moll Flanders*, 1722) the heroes of his novels. Literary characters had choices to make and through them readers experienced other lives vicariously and identified with their moral dilemmas. Though Puritans condemned novels as a pack of lies, the somewhat ingenuous defence that they were morally improving ensured their survival.

The new novel also dealt with the contemporary world: it did not look back as medieval romances and histories did, nor describe a static, unchanging universe. Reformers believed in progress, in improving society morally, culturally and technologically. This requires constant adjustment and describing the changes and their effects, whether good or bad, has kept novelists in advances, sales and royalties for centuries. The financial aspect of the literary trade may also be regarded as a consequence of the Protestant work ethic.

74. The Peace of Augsberg Seemed Like a Good Idea at the Time

Until unification in 1871 the region of present-day Germany consisted of over 300 entities ranging from large states to single towns. Due to conquests and strategic marriage alliances, individual rulers might control places hundreds of miles apart, which made keeping in touch problematic. The Catholic Holy Roman Empire owned a number of territories, as well as claiming ultimate lordship over the whole region. As Protestant ideas spread, some regions plumped for the Lutheran model, but most places remained Roman Catholic. Though some princes were undoubtedly converted to the new beliefs, others espoused Protestantism as a form of rebellion against the Habsburgs. Charles V, the current Holy Roman Emperor, tried to defuse the resulting religious and political conflict by setting up a series of consultations, starting in 1548. Like many politicians he must have hoped people would lose interest, but by 1555 an alliance of Protestant princes, the Schmalkaldic League, had had enough of this prevarication and forced an agreement.

They came up with a mission statement: *cuius regio, euis regio* (whose realm, his religion), which might be more approximately translated as 'love me, love my religion'. The rulers agreed that it would be up to them to decide the religion to which the inhabitants of their individual realms would have to subscribe. Anyone who didn't agree would be given time to migrate to a place where the ruler's beliefs tallied with their own. This was the really radical option: usually it was death to those who failed to conform. It sounded sensible at the time, even enlightened by the standards of the day, but it brought problems, as the history of the county of Lingen in Saxony illustrates. Its ruler Konrad, Count of Tecklenburg, introduced Lutheranism in 1541. In 1578 it came under the rule of the Dutch House of Orange, who imported their Calvinism. Lingen was next conquered by the Spanish in 1605 and Catholicism was imposed. When the Dutch reconquered it in 1633, Calvinism was restored. This time the population rebelled: they had had enough. They decided they liked being Catholic and forced the Prince of Orange to back down. The need to check who was in charge in order to know which religion was flavour of the month was repeated in many places and not all had such a peaceable outcome as in Lingen.

The agreement also failed to take into account the schisms within Protestantism. In 1555 only two schools of belief, Catholic and Lutheran, were envisaged. At this time Calvinism and Anabaptism were regarded as the ravings of fringe lunatics that would soon die out, but they and other reformed sects quickly attracted sizeable followings with local influence and power. As well as leading to unsettling migrations as families relocated to live in territories sympathetic to their beliefs, the Peace of Augsberg was a sticking plaster on a gaping wound, which, in 1648, broke out in to the destructive Thirty Years War. It was too reasonable, yet too prescriptive, to suit the extremism of the times.

75. THIRTY YEARS OF WAR WERE TRIGGERED BY A WINDOW IN PRAGUE

The Thirty Years War (1616–48) was the nastiest of the European Wars of Religion, a hotly contested title. It was a series of conflicts between Protestants and Catholics waged across central Europe, mainly in the area occupied by present-day Germany. Until unification in 1871 Germany was a collection of myriad states and statelets, some, like Prussia or Saxony, the size of a country, others, like Bremen, a single town under the rule of an individual lord or bishop. They were more or less all under the lordship of the Holy Roman Empire based in Austria. As the Reformation began to take hold across these territories some rulers converted to Protestantism, while many of their subjects remained Catholic. Other rulers remained Catholic and found their Protestant subjects in rebellion against them. Isolated acts of aggression on both sides soon escalated and in 1618 full-scale war erupted.

It was triggered in Bohemia, part of the present-day Czech Republic, when Matthias, the Catholic Holy Roman Emperor, wanted to ensure that his equally devout successor would be elected to the crowns of Bohemia and Hungary. Protestant leaders in Bohemia had a rival candidate who shared their faith, but the emperor prevailed. However, in 1618 Protestants threw his Catholic representatives out of a palace window. Known as the Defenestration of Prague, this set off armed conflict, although the unfortunate men survived. Initially a local Catholic v. Protestant match, it soon morphed and spread into a political, continent-wide struggle for control, or independence from an external sovereign power (mainly the Holy Roman Empire). To defend their own religion and territorial ambitions, other monarchs joined in. Even the Islamic Ottoman Empire based in Turkey became involved on the Protestant side. At one time or another, Spain, Denmark, France, the Netherlands, Russia, Poland and Sweden were also drawn in, supporting or opposing the Holy Roman Empire. England avoided major involvement, but did contribute troops.

The war had devastating effects. Some places lost up to 75 per cent of their population as warfare moved back and forth across the same stretch of land. People were not just killed in battles: it was generally starvation and disease that carried off the peasantry, as soldiers stripped the land of food and spread illness. The soldiers themselves starved. Finally the intervention of the Swedes on the Protestant side tipped the balance and brought the generation-long struggle to an end with the Peace of Westphalia, a series of treaties. Spain formally recognised the Netherlands' independence and many territorial boundaries were redrawn. It also mandated religious tolerance: Protestants and Catholics were to be equal in the eyes of the law. This was the last major conflict fought on religious grounds in Europe. Recovery took some time, not only to repair the damage to land and settlements but also to recover from depopulation. War is costly and individual nations found themselves deeply in debt or impoverished. It also changed the balance of power within Europe: the decline of Spanish influence dates from this point.

76. Islam Helped Protestantism to Survive in Europe

While Catholics and Protestants were fighting in Europe, another religion was aiming to increase its territory. The Ottoman Empire was not backward in exploiting the religious and political turmoil in Europe created by the Reformation. It was based in Constantinople, at the crossroads between Europe and Asia, and had been extending into Europe since the mid-fifteenth century. It was at the height of its power in the sixteenth century. The Turks ruled a swathe of North Africa and parts of southern Europe, including Greece and the Balkans, most of Hungary and some of the Ukraine, and was busy trying to move north. It wasn't just territory the Turks were interested in. They regularly made forays over their borders in search of Christian slaves. The Muslim Barbary pirates captured seamen in the Mediterranean and even raided isolated villages in England, Wales and Ireland for slaves who could be sold or ransomed. Although the Ottomans had arguably the better-equipped army, they would probably not have got so far had the Europeans been less busy fighting among themselves.

The main burden of driving back the Ottoman encroachments fell on the Holy Roman Emperor, just at the point when Charles V was struggling against various German princes who were converting to Protestantism. In 1523 Vienna was next on the Turks' wishlist and they laid siege to it. The weather drove them away, but the threat remained. It was a close call, but Charles decided it was more important to defeat the latter Muslims than the Protestants. Through gritted teeth he must have admitted the least were Christians.

His only big victory against the Lutherans occurred in 1547 because Suleiman, the Ottoman Emperor, was sidetracked by war in Persia.

Although he too wanted to keep the Ottomans out of Europe, Martin Luther had been a lot warmer towards Islam than towards either Catholicism ('anti-Christ') or Judaism ('the Devil'). Protestant states, like England, maintained cordial relations with the Muslims, stressing their two religions' agreement on not worshipping idols in contrast to Catholic practices. The Ottomans offered troops to the Dutch and in the 1570s the Moriscos and Protestants in Spain were negotiating to fight together. Although neither plan came to fruition, these strategies were enough to rattle Charles V.

Despite their declared Catholicism, the French gleefully encouraged the Turks to attack and allowed them to use their ports to wage war against Charles V in the Mediterranean. The Spanish Habsburg branch of the Holy Roman Empire was distracted from its anti-Protestant campaign in the Low Countries by the necessity of fighting off Islam, with French support, in a series of naval battles.

Between the siege of Vienna in 1523 and 1606, when the Treaty of Zsitva-Torok brought conflict to an end for over ninety years, a large proportion of the Holy Roman Empire's efforts and resources went into fighting the Ottomans. Without the need to keep Islam at bay the empire might have deployed all this manpower and equipment to succeed in extirpating Protestantism from Europe.

77. The Great Fire of London Fuelled Paranoia Against Foreigners

When a careless baker's oven caught fire in the night of 2 September 1666 it didn't seem like a big deal. In a city where most of the houses were still made of wood and thatched with reeds, fires were commonplace. The 100 or so parish churches all kept leather buckets and poles to pull down buildings to make firebreaks and citizens were ready to respond. But they needed leadership, and the mayor, Thomas Bloodworth, failed to rise to the occasion. 'Pish! A woman could piss it out,' he said as he hastily decamped. His actions, or rather lack of them, undoubtedly led to the fire getting out of hand. This small domestic blaze was fanned by high winds and fed by the oils, fats and other chemicals used in the many businesses located neat its artbreak. It became a firestorm, lasting three days and destroying great swathes of the city, rendering thousands homeless.

The presses of the only newspaper of the day, the *London Gazette*, were destroyed in the fire. Without official or indeed any accurate news rumours spread like, well, wildfire. Some claimed that Charles II himself was taking revenge for the execution of his father. But, as always, the main suspects were foreigners. The Anglo-Dutch War was in full swing, so it was the French and Dutch who were blamed. There were substantial communities of both nationalities in the city. Most were Protestant refugees from religious persecution, but this cut little ice with homeless people or with the anti-Catholic party who saw this as a propaganda gift. Groups of people had taken refuge in open land outside the city, and when light was seen in the sky over Fleet Street a conspiracy theorist spread the story that 50,000 immigrants were marching on Moorfields to follow up their arson with murder, rape and pillaging. A mob returned to the city to hunt down these foreigners and it took the militia and the army to push them back. But the stories seemed to be confirmed when a Frenchman, Robert Hubert, confessed he was a spy and an agent for the Pope. Then he claimed he had started the fire in Westminster and changed his story when told the fire had begun in Pudding Lane. Despite the contradictions in his account and doubts about his mental state, he was tried at the Old Bailey and convicted. After he was hanged, it emerged that he was not even in the country when the fire broke out.

When the Monument was erected in 1668 a plaque on one side recorded that this fire was 'begun and carried on by the treachery and malice of the Popish faction', adding, 'Popish frenzy which wrought such horrors, is not yet quenched.' During James II's reign (1685–89) it was removed. Although by then it was well recognised that the fire was the result of human error compounded by natural misfortunes, the plaque was reinstated following James's deposition and remained there until 1830, a daily reminder and fuelling of prejudice and paranoia.

78. Two Failed Vicars Created the Biggest Anti-Catholic Scare in English History

Throughout the seventeenth century English people saw Catholic conspiracies everywhere. Titus Oates was the origin of the largest and most extensive of them, which started in 1678. Oates's career as an Anglican priest was punctuated by accusations of perjury and sodomy (then a capital offence). Then he became a Catholic. After time spent at Jesuit establishments in France (from which he was expelled), and Spain, he returned to Britain and claimed he had pretended to convert in order to uncover Catholic secrets. With Israel Tonge, an embittered vicar whose church had been destroyed in the Great Fire of London, he concocted a document purporting to show that the Catholic Church was planning to assassinate the king. It named over 100 Jesuits and was hidden in a doctor's house, where Tonge pretended to find it. He showed it to a gullible acquaintance of the king, and an investigation was launched. Tonge and Oates were summoned.

Before giving evidence, Oates had to swear an oath before the magistrate and MP Sir Edmund Berry Godfrey. He claimed he had been present at a meeting of Jesuits at which potential methods of assassination were discussed. He was brought before Charles II. While all about him were losing their heads and running round screaming, 'Papist Plot!' the king questioned Oates closely – and became convinced he was lying. He had to agree to a full-scale enquiry, however, because it was possible that there might be some conspiracy.

Oates named more and more people, some of whom were very close to the king. Then Sir Edmund Berry

Godfrey was found murdered on Primrose Hill (this remains unsolved). Oates seized on this as proof of his claims and named more and more eminent people as perpetrators. A number of Catholics were arrested. Panic-stricken, Parliament passed an Act excluding Catholics from both Houses of Parliament, which lasted until 1829. Catholics were also forbidden to come any closer than ten miles to London. Oates was given a room in the Palace of Whitehall, a generous allowance and listened to with respect. Throughout all the hysteria, Charles II kept his head, pointing out the flaws in Oates's claims, but this did not stem trials and executions over the next three years. At least twenty-two people died in England and Ireland (Scotland remained immune) before public opinion began to turn against Oates in 1681.

When he was thrown out of his Whitehall apartment Oates denounced the king and his brother the Duke of York, which resulted in a trial for sedition. He was fined £100,000 and imprisoned. The Duke of York never forgot Oates. When he acceded to the throne in 1685 as James II, Oates was tried for perjury. As well as being whipped twice through London, he was sentenced to life imprisonment and to be put in the pillory every year. But in this case life only meant three years: when Protestant William III came to the throne in 1688, Oates was pardoned and given a pension, which he collected until his death in 1705.

79. Louis XIV's Mistress Was to Blame for the Revocation of the Edict of Nantes

Françoise d'Aubigné, Madame, then Marquise, de Maintenon, was raised as a Protestant. Her conversion to Catholicism was partly a career move but, like so many converts, she became a fervent believer. She was not keen on sex, but agreed with her confessor that becoming the latest in a long line of mistresses to Louis XIV would be an opportunity to steer the old rake in a more godly direction. When Louis revoked the Edict of Nantes in 1685 it was said by her enemies that she and his Jesuit confessor had cooked up the scheme as a penance for the king to atone for his libertine ways. Satirical pamphlets spread claims that the Revocation was her price for agreeing to a clandestine marriage to the king and that she had persuaded his confessor to co-operate.

Louis, however, was an absolute autocrat. For him there were two opinions on everything: his own, and the wrong one. Françoise had been his illegitimate children's governess and she was always aware of her subservience. The privileges accorded Protestants by the Edict of Nantes in 1598 had been gradually eroded for many years before Françoise appeared on the scene. Although she welcomed Protestant conversions, she did not approve of the violent *dragonnades* launched in 1681 at Louis's instigation. Victorian historians, both French and British, were particularly happy to ascribe good decisions to their heroes but claim that bad decisions (and the Revocation was not sensible) were due to feminine influence. Their prejudices have cast a long shadow.

80. THE FALL OF LA ROCHELLE SOUNDED THE DEATH KNELL OF PROTESTANTS IN FRANCE

Henri IV (1553–1610) ended the French Wars of Religion in 1598 by signing the Edict of Nantes, which gave toleration to Protestants – an astonishingly liberal gesture for that time. Although it confirmed that the Catholic Church was paramount, Protestants were granted fortified 'places of safety', most notably La Rochelle, which the Crown paid to maintain, and some 150 other sites paid for by the Protestants themselves. Although they had freedom of conscience, they were permitted to worship as they wished only in specified places. The right to work for the state and in all professions was also affirmed. Protestants were allowed to bring grievances directly to the king, bypassing local authorities, which gave them privileges denied to others. In the teeth of opposition from regional parliaments, which could accept or reject edicts, a tenuous acceptance was reached. By allowing Protestants their own towns and autonomy in other matters, Henri created what was virtually an alternative state within France – so he sowed the seeds of disaster in the future. La Rochelle was a busy seaport on the Atlantic: handing over control of it had economic and strategic implications.

After Henri's assassination in 1610, it was not long before his successors began to chip away the provisions of the Edict, initially triggered by Protestant uprisings in the south during the 1620s. These were supported by England. In 1627 La Rochelle was besieged for fourteen months. Although the English attempted unsuccessfully to send in men and supplies to their co-religionists, the Protestant Dutch government rented ships to the French to transport their troops. Louis XIII was victorious and the places the Protestants governed were limited to two: La Rochelle and Montauban.

The episode demonstrated to the French Crown that it was impossible to tolerate Protestants running what was effectively a parallel administration, even in limited areas. They effectively formed a fifth column within the country with links to overseas enemies, like England, and they openly resented rule by Catholics. The right of the various Protestant towns to be fortified was removed because the possibilities of armed rebellion would be ever-present. The Crown tightened and centralised its grip on government, producing the absolutism that reached its apogee in Louis XIV, a man for whom the label 'control freak' is a massive understatement. When he came to the throne in 1661, 300 families were expelled from La Rochelle, where local Catholics resented their increasing ownership of property and businesses.

Over the years the right to hold professional positions was removed and places of worship were pulled down, usually on health-and-safety grounds. Only freedom of worship was retained. Still Protestantism remained uneradicated, so in 1681 Louis imposed the *dragonnades*. Mounted soldiers were billeted on Protestants, who had to support them at their own expense. So aggressive were the dragoons that a major exodus began. Then, in 1685, Louis finally revoked the Edict of Nantes and declared open season on Protestants.

81. French Protestants Saw Off the Last English Catholic Monarch

James II, openly Catholic, succeeded his brother Charles II, secretly Catholic, as King of England and was crowned in February 1685. He was keen to extend tolerance of Catholics and Nonconformists in England, but was distinctly intolerant towards Presbyterians north of the border in Scotland, where he was King James VII. This caused English suspicions that he was proposing tolerance of Nonconformists to mask a cunning plan to bring back Catholic supremacy in Britain. Rebellions against him in Scotland and in the West of England soon after his coronation were defeated, but when he increased the size of the standing army and appointed some Catholic generals this was taken by the more panicky Protestants in the government as evidence that he was planning a military coup.

His downfall resulted from French Protestants. From 1681 increased persecution in France had been bringing a flood of Huguenots to England. Most of them arrived in London, joining the community established by refugees from earlier waves. In October 1685 the Edict of Nantes was revoked and even more arrived, bringing with them horror stories of having their children forcibly taken from them, of execution, torture, imprisonment and loss of lands and money. Their experiences seemed a foretaste of Catholic rule in England but James saw no reason to soft pedal. A month after the Revocation he prorogued Parliament to rule alone and began to drive through his plans to extend religious liberty to Catholics.

As long as James had only daughters – Mary and Anne, by his first wife – the ruling classes thought this might just be bearable. Both women had been brought up as Protestants and, their gardes dictated that they must obey their husbands regardless, so when James died someone more malleable could be put on the throne. Then the king remarried and his second wife gave birth to a son in 1688. Stories that the baby was smuggled in to the birthing chamber in a warming pan failed to gain credence and so the game changed.

Desperate Huguenot refugees were still arriving in their thousands, with lurid experiences of life under a Catholic king. James might be regarded as unlucky, but it was his lack of political sense that led to his downfall. He had learned nothing from the fate of his father, Charles I (another Catholic with a belief in the divine right of kings), who had disrespected Parliament and had his head cut off. He failed to understand the propaganda value of these asylum seekers from France and the stories of their sufferings.

Plans to replace James with his son-in-law William of Orange had been formulated when the queen's pregnancy because known, and when a son was born they swung into action. James escaped his father's fate and fled to France, to England's old enemy and the persecutor of the Huguenots whose plight had brought him down. This only confirmed what many English people believed he had planned for them. James II and his descendants made attempts to recover the throne, but he was the last Roman Catholic King of England.

82. The Battle of the Boyne in 1690 Marks the Triumph of Protestantism in Britain

The Glorious Revolution of 1688 is usually considered to be when Protestantism was finally secured as the state religion in Britain. Catholic King James II was painlessly deposed in favour of his daughter Mary and Dutch son-in-law, William of Orange. Although there were riots in London there are few landmarks in English history without some civil uproar in the capital. Serious threats to the new king came mainly from France, where James had taken refuge. Louis XIV hadn't bothered much about William's takeover, which he thought would provoke civil war. When this did not materialise he saw restoring James as a way both of securing Catholicism in Britain and extending his political power over his old enemy – not necessarily in that order of importance.

In 1689 Louis sent troops to Ireland with James. This was partly to support James's attempt to regain the throne and partly to draw William III away from the Netherlands so that the French could move in there. The Pope, alarmed by Louis's ambitions, backed Protestant William, to whom he gave his blessing. Maybe this tipped the balance: William defeated James at the decisive Battle of the Boyne in July 1690.

Although many historians regard William's accession in 1688 as the crucial date, and Bonnie Prince Charlie might have been a threat in 1745, on balance 1690 is the year that should be remembered as the date when Protestantism was finally secured as the state religion of England. The later Act of Union in 1707, which joined Scottish Presbyterianism to English and Welsh Protestantism, created a united front.

83. THE BANK OF ENGLAND WAS FOUNDED BY HUGUENOTS

An estimated 200,000 Protestant refugees fled France following the Revocation of the Edict of Nantes in 1685 when practising their religion became illegal. Some 50,000 pitched up in Britain and contributed significantly to its prosperity. Although best remembered as silkweavers in Spitalfields in London, their skills and influence spread across all levels of society. And so did their money. Many had managed to bring with them substantial sums and they set about investing it in new businesses in their adopted land. Among the organisations they are credited with founding is the Bank of England. This was established in 1694 during a war with the usual adversary: France. William III needed cash to rebuild the navy, but no one was prepared to lend him money because they were afraid he'd default on any loan and, being the king, could say, 'So sue me,' with impunity. What he needed was his very own bank, and he needed £1.5 million (about £2.5 billion today) to start it. A whip-round produced this sum. William was prepared to pay 8 per cent interest (an excellent return and a sign of his desperation) and some 1,272 people thought this was worth a flutter. Among these initial investors were a number of Huguenots and those of Huguenot descent. As well as getting a good return on their money, they would be supporting the war against their persecutor Louis XIV and the religion he was hoping to export to Britain.

Twenty-four prominent men were chosen to run this new bank, which would act as the English government's banker. Seven of these twenty-four were of Huguenot descent, including the first governor, Sir John Houblon (1632–1712), a descendant of Protestant refugees from Flanders who arrived in Elizabeth I's reign. His investment was £10,000, and other members of his family also paid in, which no doubt influenced his appointment. Although it was not Huguenots alone who founded the Bank of England, their role and financial support were essential in getting it off the ground.

Huguenot influence was not confined to the bank itself. From 1724 banknotes have been produced on paper made by a company near Southampton created by Henri de Portal. Family legend says that young Henri and his brother were smuggled out of France in winecasks and landed in Southampton, where they joined the local Huguenot community. The lad had to ditch his aristocratic expectations of an easy life and get a job in a local papermill. He learned fast and founded a family business that was finally sold to the De La Rue company in 1995. The company still produces banknotes and security papers for passports and other documents for over 150 countries, including Britain. The pounds in your wallet, as well as those in the Bank of England, originated with Huguenot investment.

84. HUGUENOTS CREATED THE IRISH LINEN INDUSTRY

Irish linen is one of the country's best-known exports and the linen industry is often attributed to Huguenots who arrived in Ireland from the latter part of the seventeenth century. When William III went on military campaign in Ireland in 1690 to defeat his deposed father-in-law, James II, he was mainly occupied with plans to prevent James leading his fellow Catholics to victory and reinstalling himself on the English throne. He was not, however, too busy to notice that Ireland had a small linen industry dating back many centuries. At this time, it was only a cottage industry: men grew the flax and their wives and children spun it and wove linen. An effort in 1632 to import Dutch flaxseed and build improved looms had foundered because people resisted the new methods. By 1697 there may have been as many as 1,000 small-scale producers scattered over various counties.

Having defeated his father-in-law, William turned his attention to his impoverished and resentful province. English woollen producers were nagging him to stop the Irish competing with them, which he did. Restricting wool manufacture increased the importance of linen in Ireland. William lifted taxes on it, but this was not enough to increase production significantly. In 1690 Huguenot Nicholas Dupin made renewed suggestions to improve manufacture. The man who usually gets the credit, however, is Louis Crommelin (1652–1727).

The Protestant Crommelin family were driven from Picardy, France following the Revocation of the Edict of Nantes (1685). They had run a textile business, but after taking refuge in Amsterdam Louis Crommelin became a partner in a bank. When William was looking for someone to bring both expertise in weaving and commercial skills to Ireland, he asked Louis if it would be possible to bring Huguenots to Ireland to teach their weaving skills to the locals. In 1698 Louis brought some seventy of his fellow countrymen and 300 looms to Lisburn. He and his son (another Louis) were dynamic businessmen and with English government grants they established a flourishing enterprise. Soon 1,000 looms were clacking away and another manufactory was established in Kilkenny, run by a Crommelin brother. Dutchmen were brought over to teach their flax-growing skills. In 1701 Louis launched another innovation, a mass bleaching site on the outskirts of Lisburn.

Improving the economy was not the only motive for bringing in Huguenots. The English government intended to spread Protestantism across its rebellious province. To this end, many of the Huguenots newly arrived from France were encouraged to settle in Ireland. This secondary motive manifestly failed. It cannot be said that the Huguenots created the linen industry in Ireland, but they transformed it from a small-scale family-based cottage industry into an efficient and major contributor to the Irish economy. By the end of the eighteenth century linen was estimated to have formed about half of the country's total exports, and is still an important product today.

85. PROTESTANTISM CREATED CAPITALISM

In 1905 Max Weber coined the phrase 'Protestant work ethic'. He argued that in Catholicism salvation comes through taking part in church services and obeying ecclesiastical authority. Although it praises ordinary labourers, the Catholic Church maintains that those whose lives are devoted to religious observance, like priests, monks and nuns, are more valuable in God's estimation. Protestants, particularly Calvinists, believe that working hard and prospering in secular trades is evidence that the individual involved is one of God's elect. This applies as equally to the industrial magnate as to the humblest factory hand; doing a job well to the best of one's ability and in praise of God is assurance of salvation. This ethic created capitalism, as purely monetary success came to be regarded as an end in itself: proof of God's approval as opposed to the concept of holy poverty promoted in Catholicism.

Historically Protestant countries, like the USA, Britain, Germany and Scandinavia, are richer and have a higher standard of living than more or less the rest of the world, whether Catholic, Islamic, Hindu, Confucian, communist or whatever, where devoting one's whole existence to religious (or, in the case of communism, political) observance is esteemed more highly than doing a mundane job, which is rather despised. However, capitalism actually began among the merchants of resolutely Catholic Italy during the fourteenth century. The decline of feudalism following the Black Death in the fourteenth century also contributed to the growth of capitalism as the dearth of serfs gave those who survived some bargaining power to negotiate financial and other benefits. Property laws, central to capitalism, were also being modified.

Although undoubtedly Calvinist beliefs did contribute to the growth of capitalist economies, other factors also played a part. Protestants were generally better educated, as being able to read the Bible was regarded as an important skill (although being able to write and disseminate radical ideas was less favoured). The emphasis on personal autonomy inherent in the belief in individual conscience led to many innovations and discoveries, which improved technology and processes in all fields. There was no need to self-censor in case an idea was deemed heretical by the Church. In many places the wrong kind of Protestants were, like Jews, excluded from important professions, especially those which were connected to government administration. Trade became the only outlet for bright, dynamic, nonconformist individuals and naturally they flourished. The most successful were able to influence their governments indirectly because of their financial muscle, like the Quakers in Britain whose banking expertise gave them considerable political clout from the eighteenth century. Weber's central thesis is partly true: the capitalism of the modern world would not have developed without Protestant beliefs, especially those of Calvinism, but it is not the sole factor.

86. The Protestant Work Ethic Created the Industrial Revolution

Catholicism is focused on the afterlife: rewards in heaven are dependent on piety on earth. Protestantism judges the state of individuals' souls by how hard they work and is mainly confined to places where it is tough to wrest a living from the land. This does not explain why England was the site of the first Industrial Revolution: Scotland and certain Swiss cantons were far more Presbyterian and their inhabitants had to work far harder against more hostile environments to earn a living. Britain, however, was blessed with the raw materials, like coal, iron and tin, which benefited manufacture. Its worldwide colonial links facilitated the purchase of cotton to be spun and the sale of finished goods. One of the theories about the origins of the Industrial Revolution in Britain focuses on the growth of the transatlantic slave trade, necessitating the production of fabrics, metalwork and firearms to trade for slaves from African chiefs – all goods which then formed the basis of Britain's worldwide trade.

Indeed Protestantism fostered a number of the ingredients needed to start a social and cultural revolution. People were encouraged to read the Bible for themselves, which increased literacy; they were expected to solve problems for themselves, including working out what to do when faced with moral dilemmas. This intellectual ingenuity could be applied to solve technological problems. The exclusion from public life of non-Anglicans meant that people of talent, drive and creativity who might have gone into unproductive government sinecures were diverted instead into business and commerce.

87. The Irish Economy Was Damaged by Wild Geese

From the mid-seventeenth to the mid-eighteenth century the exodus from France by persecuted French Protestants was matched by a large section of the Irish Catholic population heading in the opposite direction to Europe, probably making rude gestures to each other as their boats crossed the Channel. These romantically named 'Wild Geese' were largely from the gentry – landowners in flight from discrimination and worse from their English rulers – but there were some aristocrats. They had been leaving since the beginning of the Reformation, but following William III's victory in Ireland in 1691 fierce anti-Catholic laws were passed. Some 15,000 soldiers were also more than encouraged to leave – no one wanted so many hardened but disgruntled military men on England's doorstep, plotting revenge and fomenting rebellions.

Hundreds found employment in the armies of mainland Europe, but some went further – in at least one case to serve in the Imperial Chinese Navy. Most went to England's traditional enemy, France, but the Spanish, Bohemian, Bavarian and Russian armies also benefited from their presence. Some individuals rose to high office. Irishmen occupied important posts in the Spanish Empire in Venezuela, Puerto Rico and other outposts. Maximilian Ulysses Browne became a Field Marshal in the Holy Roman Empire. Below them were many hundreds in the rank and file. The political state of eighteenth-century Europe meant that Irish people on both sides often wound up fighting each other, as Browne did against the Spanish Irish Brigade in 1744. It was not just Scots who supported the claim of the Old and Young Pretenders in the early eighteenth century. Irish exiles also made no secret of their desire to see the Stuarts restored to the British throne. Bonnie Prince Charlie was so heartened by their willingness to fight for his cause that he launched his uprising in 1745. Both France and Spain declared war on Britain and sided with America during the War of Independence. Their Irish Brigades fought the British.

It was not just military men who went overseas. Irish merchants, doctors and administrators all headed off, keen to practise their religion freely. Undoubtedly the departure of so many of these talented people damaged Ireland as much as the Huguenot emigration from France damaged that country's economy. The English and later British governments poured money into trying to improve the Irish economy, but it was the lack of a skilled middle-class that was decisive. The decline began long before the Irish Potato Famine drove thousands more abroad. Many never gave up hope that they would be able to return. The first generation or two continued to speak Gaelic, but quickly English became the lingua franca, and then the local language became the only one they understood. Like their Protestant counterparts in Britain, most settled down, assimilated and became part of the societies in which they lived, with just an occasional reminder of their roots, like celebrating St Patrick's Day with considerably more fervour than their neighbours.

88. The End of the Reformation Meant Monasteries Were Safe from Suppression

It was not only in Britain that monasteries were suppressed or dissolved. Many across Europe also disappeared, initially from Protestant states. In many Swiss cantons before the Reformation, monasteries were under secular supervision and education was managed by lay authorities, although teachers were generally priests. As might be expected, it was the Swiss city-state of Zurich, the home of influential reformer Huldrich Zwingli, that was first off the block in the race to suppress monastic life completely. Zurich was followed by Basel in 1529 and Geneva in 1530. The declared motive for the dissolution was to use the wealth of the establishments to educate and care for the poor. Some cantons, however, remained Catholic and kept their religious houses.

The next rulers to appropriate the wealth of the monasteries were Gustav Vasa of Sweden in 1527 and Frederick I of Denmark in 1528, who openly stated they thought the religious houses were a waste of money. They confiscated some establishments for their own enrichment and ownership of others was passed to noblemen who supported them – particularly important in Gustav's case. The process was fairly bloodless in Denmark and its territories of Norway and Iceland. Priests, monks and nuns were allowed to stay in their churches, monasteries and convents. When they died they were not replaced, so the institutions simply withered away. This also gave ordinary people time to adjust to the new order. These precedents might have given Henry VIII some useful tips when he started his campaign in 1536.

Like Switzerland, Germany was a collection of independent territories. It was not until 1648, at the end of the Thirty Years War, that the rulers of Protestant areas were able to begin the process of confiscating monastic lands and revenues. Compared to other places the toll here – just over 100 – was relatively modest, and the rulers, like Philip of Hesse and Maurice of Saxony, mainly used the money raised to improve education for Lutherans, which must have rubbed salt into wounds. In central Europe religious houses suffered when countries like Bohemia changed hands: Protestants suppressed them, Catholics re-established them.

By 1780 monks and nuns must have thought they were safe from ejection from their monasteries and convents. But Joseph II, ruler of the staunchly Catholic Holy Roman Empire, dissolved more than 600 monasteries in the parts of Germany, Austria and Hungary that he controlled. His motives were neither religious nor monetary. Influenced by the rationalism introduced by the Enlightenment, he decided that the contemplative orders were useless; only those that benefited the community by teaching, nursing or other practical work should continue. The money from these dissolutions would go to support more parish priests. The nineteenth century saw further suppressions, this time for political reasons, in France, Italy, Spain, Switzerland, Hungary and Lithuania. Only Austria hung on to the establishments that survived Joseph II. In the twentieth century religious houses in countries under communist rule suffered, but a lack of vocations among believers has further dwindled numbers.

89. THE ENLIGHTENMENT BROUGHT THE REFORMATION TO AN END

Naturally the French claim they began the Enlightenment, more precisely called the Age of Reason, which started shortly after the start of the Reformation. The French say this was the brainchild of René Descartes (1596–1650), who published a method of reasoning encapsulated in his dictum, 'I think therefore I am,' but there is a better case to be made for two medieval Englishmen, Robert Grosseteste and Roger Bacon, who, in the thirteenth century, described applying scientific methods of empirical observation and reason to the world about them rather than relying on what had previously been written on a subject. They were not much regarded: people were taught that knowledge was fixed, unchangeable and contained in the texts approved by the Catholic Church.

The most influential early scientists, such as Francis Bacon (1562–1626) and Isaac Newton (1642–1727), worked in Protestant societies: the Reformers' constant search to discover truth, to weigh one Biblical injunction against another, influenced their thought processes. Francis Bacon's contemporary, the Italian Galileo Galilei (1564–1642), used observation and reason to confirm Nicholas Copernicus's theory that the sun, not the earth, was the centre of the solar system. The Catholic Church insisted that the earth was the centre of the entire universe and Galileo fell foul of the Inquisition. Under threat of torture he recanted. His fate was a warning to other Catholics who might have considered using scientific reason rather than toe the official line. Although Galileo recanted he is said to have muttered, 'But it still moves.' The Church might be able to force an old man to deny what he knew to be true but it could not change the laws of nature, and by the Counter-Reformation it had to accept the validity of scientific observation and its conclusions.

All religion is based on faith – belief without any empirical evidence – so the scientific advances that questioned what had previously been accepted unthinkingly inevitably led to questions about religious, political and economic assumptions. This lead to questioning the authority of the Catholic Church. Here the French *philosophes* were strongly represented and they spread their ideas and arguments for scientific methods of enquiry and toleration of religion, playing cat and mouse with the Catholic authorities until the French Revolution in 1789. It became clear during the early eighteenth century that religious conversion would have to be on the basis of persuasion rather than external force, and the rulers of most European nations, whether Protestant or Catholic, became more or less tolerant of difference of opinion.

Whether it was the spirit and successes of the Age of Reason that brought to an end the religious wars and massacres that marked the period of the Reformation remains an open question, unprovable by scientific method. Even today there are communities, like Ireland, in which Christian religious affiliation matters. Although fewer and fewer people identify themselves as having a formal religious faith, not everyone yet lives solely by scientific reason, so the Enlightenment, like the Reformation, has not finished its stated work.

90. WILDCARDS 3: QUAKERS

The Religious Society of Friends (Quakers) was founded by George Fox, who reckoned neither the Church of England nor the Calvinist reformers had got it right. He had a vision on Pendle Hill, Lancashire, which prompted him to spread the word that believers could have a direct experience of Christ without guidance from ministers. He was lucky not to have faced trial as a witch – ten women who lived around Pendle Hill were hanged for witchcraft in 1612. Fortunately for him, by 1650 matters had calmed down in the demon-hunting business and he was just brought before magistrates and charged with blasphemy. He told them they should tremble at the word of the Lord and one of the magistrates called his followers Quakers in mockery. The name stuck, both with the mockers and with those who were converted. The movement quickly grew, despite persecution, which did not officially end until 1689. They were regarded as dangerously idealistic extremists: pacifists in a time of continuous wars; they refused to swear oaths on the Bible in a time when it was believed that not to do so invited divine wrath; and, horror of horrors, they allowed and even encouraged *women* to preach. Spiritual equality of the sexes in God's sight was definitely eccentric. In practice, unconventionality would only go so far: women had separate meetings which confined them to the traditional activities of charitable work, especially among children.

In England and Wales membership peaked in the early 1680s, partly because so many Quakers – like William Penn, who founded Pennsylvania in 1682 – saw the Americas as a haven in which to build a society run on religious lines, and decamped there. The introduction of a veto on marrying outside the society undoubtedly caused losses but internal dissent, conducted quietly and with 'holy conversation' as befitted such a seemly organisation, also led to a reduction in their numbers about this time. However, they built up an influence disproportionate to their membership; their moral principles meant that they were trusted in business, which led to economic success, particularly in banking. They ejected businessmen whose companies failed if they were deemed to have acted unwisely, which was and remains an exceptional example. The abolition of the European slave trade and slavery in the colonies might not have happened when it did without the determined campaigns of Quakers around the globe at a time when slavery was regarded as both Biblically sanctioned and financially profitable. To sacrifice profit for moral principle was seen as wilfully eccentric.

They adopted the name Religious Society of Friends in the nineteenth century, when they were keen to be seen as the solid, respectable members of society they had become, rather than the lunatics on the fringe of popular imagination they had been in previous centuries. Today their principles are deeply respected. Even if, like pacifism, some remain impractical in today's world, Quakers remain moral exemplars and a reminder of what might be achieved by thinking outside of the box.

91. THE OLD AND YOUNG PRETENDERS MADE SCOTLAND MORE PROTESTANT

When he was deposed from the English throne in 1688, James II took refuge with his wife and son in France. His descendants grew up convinced they'd been robbed and that it was their destiny to return Britain to Catholicism. James's son, another James, and grandson Charles are known as the Old and Young Pretender. Their attempts to recover the throne show that some people never learn and further entrenched Protestantism in Scotland.

In 1708 James made his first attempt, The Old Pretender to reclaim the crown, supported by Louis XIV, who was never reluctant to annoy the English. The admiral of the French ships was too afraid of the British navy and retreated. In 1715 some Scots rebelled and this time James did land, but he failed to attract enough support. On his return to France he was deemed an embarrassment and exiled to Italy, but his attempts had revealed a residue of support for the Stuarts in Scotland. In 1745 his son Charles made a better attempt to restore the family fortunes. Catholicism was still widespread among the clans in the Scottish Highlands, and even some Protestant clans there supported the Stuarts' claim. With French backing Charles landed in Scotland and initially did well. Edinburgh surrendered, he won a number of battles and got as far south as Carlisle, but the hoped-for English support never materialised. Reluctantly he led his army back to Scotland, where the Battle of Culloden proved disastrous. Charles fled from the carnage. His escape from Scotland back to France is a romantic tale of derring-do which became the stuff of legends. But the pragmatic French found his failure just as embarrassing as his father's had been and expelled him in 1748. Telling himself that the restoration of the Stuarts was more important than religion, he declared himself willing to convert to Protestantism, even taking Anglican Communion during a secret visit to London in 1750. When this failed to win him support, he returned to Catholicism.

In 1759 the French called him in, planning to use his Highland supporters as part of an invasion for their own purposes, but his demands and lack of realism quickly caused them to drop him. The final chance had slipped away. When died in 1766 The Old Pretender Charles decided to call himself Charles III, but no one else did. Even the Pope refused to recognise his claim and the twenty-two remaining years of his life were spent drifting, dependent on handouts.

The Presbyterians in the Scottish Parliament were so infuriated by the display of Catholic strength he had revealed that they expelled moderate Episcopalians (conformists to Anglicanism) for fear they might let in Catholicism by the back door. From afar Charles must have seen how his father and grandfather's failed attempts and his own defeat had actually further entrenched fundamental Protestantism in Scotland.

92. ANTI-CATHOLIC PREJUDICE CONTINUED IN THE ROYAL FAMILY FOR OVER 400 YEARS

The first head of the Church of England, Henry VIII, did not have a good track record producing descendants. All three of his children died without heirs, so his great-great-nephew James VI of Scotland inherited the English throne. James proved good at procreating and his direct descendants occupied the throne until 1688 (with only a slight hiccup when Charles I was executed by the Puritan Commonwealth). In 1688 James II was deposed because of his Catholic sympathies. His daughters, Mary and Anne, occupied the throne in succession, but had no surviving children, and in 1701 panic broke out. James II had attempted an armed invasion to take back what he regarded as his rightful inheritance and, more provocatively, to reimpose Catholicism. On his death in 1701 his son's claim was endorsed by the Pope. The fact that the exiled Stuarts had French support did not endear them to the Francophobic English either.

The fear that the Reformation's work would be undone led to the passing of the Act of Settlement in 1701. It laid down that on the death of Queen Anne the crown would pass to the Electress Sophia of Hanover – one of fertile James I's grandchildren – and her heirs, so long as they were not Catholics. Anyone who became a Roman Catholic or married one would be automatically disbarred from the throne. The Act also limited the role foreigners could play in Parliament. Though this was amended by subsequent legislation, the veto on Catholics becoming or being married to a monarch of Britain remained on the statute books. This was somewhat based on the fear that future monarchs would be seduced by pillow talk into embracing Roman Catholicism and its supposed errors. Though prejudice and immediate political factors were probably uppermost in the government's thinking, there was a further consideration. The Church of England was, and still is, the established Church – part of government. In 1688 the monarch's coronation oath was rewritten with significant alterations. Previously laws were described being enacted 'through the King's grant' but William III and Mary II were required to obey the laws passed by Parliament. They also had to maintain 'the true Profession of the Gospel and the Protestant Reformed Religion Established by Law', rather than making a vague promise to support bishops. Anyone who could not do this would cause massive constitutional problems.

Since then each monarch has sworn to uphold the Protestant religion with no crises of conscience, but a number of royals have opted for love rather than a place in the long queue for the throne by marrying a Catholic or converting. The Succession to the Crown Act 2013, brought into force on 26 March 2015, finally ended this dilemma. A person who marries a Roman Catholic will no longer be disqualified from the line of succession. However, the first six persons in line to the throne (as required by the Royal Marriage Act of 1772) still need to seek the sovereign's approval to marry. So far their choices have seemed eminently suitable.

93. English University Education Was Improved by Dissent

Until the mid-nineteenth century Oxford and Cambridge were the only universities in England, and from 1662 onwards those who wished to study at Oxford or to graduate from both universities were required to subscribe to the truth of the Church of England's central doctrines. This sneakily excluded Catholics and dissenters from higher education and the networking opportunities that Oxbridge has always offered without actually forbidding them from getting a degree or influential contacts. Women, whatever their religion, were of course rejected. Catholics who could afford to mainly sent their sons abroad. Many nonconformist ministers, not allowed to preach, turned to teaching – the default occupation of many people who can't find another job – but from these unpromising beginnings a superior form of education emerged.

Parents whose nonconformist religious affiliations made Oxbridge unthinkable and who couldn't afford overseas study sent their sons to learn from those who shared their beliefs. Some ministers simply took a few pupils into their homes, but others set up academies offering a university-level curriculum. They might be supported by their denomination's central body, which also offered grants to poor students. The focus was on preparing people for the ministry, but over the course of the eighteenth century the field of studies widened.

Oxbridge had grown complacent. With a monopoly in educating the offspring of the upper classes, who were there primarily to learn how to run the country, not much useful research got done. Tutors amused themselves with internal and external politics, took advantage of the generous free meals at High Table and did a little light teaching when all else failed. There were exceptions, like Isaac Newton at Cambridge and Edmund Halley of comet fame at Oxford, but in general the upsurge in scientific interest sparked by the Enlightenment passed the two universities by. This was another reason for parents to look elsewhere. Barred from many positions, nonconformists went into trade and industry and they needed their children to be educated in science, technology and innovation. They did not want dead languages like Greek and Latin, but thriving ones like German and French to deal with customers and to keep up with foreign competition. They needed geography, not a history of Caesar's Gallic Wars.

In 1826 London University opened but this provocative title was challenged by Oxbridge's vested interests and it was renamed University College London. It was soon followed by King's College London in 1829. Both delivered non-denominational education in modern subjects and formed the basis of the collection of institutions, including the medical schools of St Thomas's Hospital and Barts that became the University of London. It took a long fight against Oxbridge and the Church of England, who wanted to preserve their iron grip, before the University of London became the third university in England, awarding its first degrees in 1839. Two dissenting academies in Manchester developed into the University of Manchester, and this pattern was repeated across the country. Without this kind of competition, Oxbridge would not have had to raise its game.

94. PROTESTANTS ENDED THE EUROPEAN TRANSATLANTIC SLAVE TRADE

In medieval Europe the Church taught that it was wrong to enslave fellow Christians but okay to enslave Muslims and pagans. Incredibly, there was some debate about whether Africans, very different in appearance to Europeans, were actually human. It was argued that dogs and cats are both furry and four-legged, with a tail and two ears, but this did not make then the same. Were Africans actually a separate species from Europeans in the way cats and dogs are different? The consensus became that they were human. Muslim Arabs had a similar view: they enslaved Christians and pagans.

When trading voyages to Africa from Portugal and Spain began in the early fifteenth century, Europeans discovered that African chiefs were happy to sell slaves to them, as they had been doing for centuries to Arab traders. This conveniently coincided with the beginnings of colonialism. Labour was needed in the new territories of the Americas and the Iberian slave-traders were soon followed by the Dutch, the French, the British, the Danes and the Swedish. For Christians, however, it created a conundrum.

Money usually trumps morality, and a cosy, economically satisfactory accord was reached. Though human, Africans were considered heathens, so they could be enslaved and transported across the Atlantic. At the other end, both Catholics and Protestants behaved hypocritically. Catholics baptised their slaves; Protestants tried to ensure their slaves did not receive religious instruction. Missionaries were discouraged and conversions largely ignored. For a few centuries this duplicity benefited the competing economies of the various European states, whatever their religion.

The spanner in the works became nonconformists. The Bible endorsed slavery, with details about how it was to be managed. Though Protestants regarded every word of the Bible as sacrosanct they never attempted to reintroduce slavery into their homelands. It contradicted their belief in the autonomy of the individual, in his (and her) ability to deal directly with God. At first individuals, like the Quaker George Fox, encouraged people to treat slaves humanely, but eventually the disquiet about enslaving fellow human beings reached critical mass. The first campaigners off the block were Quakers in England and the historically Protestant states of New England, who began the fight in the 1750s. They were joined by people of other Protestant denominations, mainly nonconformist, but later Anglican and Lutheran, for whom their conscience was more important than the snare of profit. It was a long, hard-fought battle against vested interests. Lutheran Denmark was actually the first state to abolish its slave trade in 1802, but as this was only a minute component of their economy it's not regarded as significant. When powerful Britain, then the leading slave-trading nation, abolished its slave trade in 1807 it set off a domino effect in both Protestant and, eventually, Catholic states, partly because it had the muscle to impose its views on other nations. Once the trade was abolished, the next fight, the abolition of the status of slavery itself in the colonies of the New World, began, and was also spearheaded by nonconformists.

95. The Creation of Belgium Had Its Roots in the Reformation

The modern state of Belgium, created in 1830, sits in a strategic location in Europe. The term 'Belgian' was used by historians to denote this area, but from medieval times the various provinces were part of the region known as the Low Countries, stretching from the modern-day Netherlands in the north to parts of present-day France in the south. The northern part was the province of Flanders and the language there was Flemish, a dialect of Dutch. The southern area, the provinces of Artois, Hainault and Cambrai, known collectively as Wallonia, spoke Walq, a dialect of French. The inhabitants, whichever language they spoke, got used to their country being a sought-after possession because it was a prosperous region with good agricultural land and at the crossroads of trade. From 1384 this hotly contested territory came under the rule of the dukes of Burgundy, who brought peace and the region flourished.

A chain of marriages, deaths and births brought the whole of the Low Countries under highly unpopular Spanish Habsburg rule in 1494. The Spanish Inquisition was introduced to crush the Reformation and the first Protestant martyrs were burned in Brussels in 1523. Rebellions started in 1559, lasting fifty years. The northern United Provinces, the present-day Netherlands, won independence in 1609, while the southern area remained Catholic under Spanish rule. This saw a massive movement of the populations of the two areas: many Protestants moved north, but far fewer Catholics moved south. Depopulation led to economic decline, to more migration, even among

Catholics, many of whom preferred financial security to religious conviction under Spanish rule.

France had always been keen to acquire this region, gobbling up provinces whenever the opportunity arose and finally annexing all the territories up to the Dutch border in 1794. Their possession was brief: the defeat of Napoleon in 1815 saw this region of Europe carved up between the victors. Flanders and Wallonia were given to the Netherlands, ruled by a Calvinist king who began a campaign against the Roman Catholic Church. In August 1830 the people rebelled. They resented being ruled by a Protestant and suffering discrimination. A revolutionary committee was formed and declared independence 'of the provinces of Belgium'. A few months later in London the Belgian Congress organised an armistice and gave the new territory a king, Leopold I of Saxe-Coburg, one of the many spare German princes floating around at the time. It also confirmed the name 'Belgium'.

Today Belgium is still culturally divided: the Protestant Flemings regard themselves as the hard-working, economic power house of the country and look down on their southern French-speaking Catholic Walloon compatriots. A split is regularly prophesied, this time not on religious grounds but on cultural grounds. Yet these two cultures are the product of the religious conflict that divided the region some 400 years ago and are still to some extent being fought out today.

96. Oliver Cromwell's Laws Lasted until the Twentieth Century

For centuries visitors, even from other Protestant countries, dreaded the British Sunday. Everywhere was closed, there was nothing to do, children were prevented from playing in the street. It was often the only day that some workers got off, but there was nothing to entertain them. Oliver Cromwell and his Puritans are often held responsible.

Even while the English Civil War was being fought, the Puritans found time to ban what they saw as remnants of Catholic practices, such as celebrations on Christmas Day, which were replaced by fasting and prayer. In between recruiting and paying the armed forces, and running a country at war, a host of bans were passed on stage plays, the Book of Sports, cockfighting (the Puritans weren't always wrong) and even on a custom of scrambling for cakes on Easter Day at the parish church in Twickenham. These ordinances were rigorously enforced during the Commonwealth period. All Holy Days were to be turned into recreation days, but the Puritan idea of recreation did not involve pleasure. Monthly fast days and days of repentance and humiliation were substituted and compulsory attendance for worship on Sunday was enforced. But with the restoration of Charles II in 1660, Sunday went back to being a day of rambunctious recreation.

It was not the Puritans but rather the passing of the Sunday Observance Act 1780 which was the real source of the dreaded British Sunday. The primary motivation behind it was political rather than religious, to limit the opportunities for dissenters and freethinkers to meet on their days off work and cause trouble. The result was to curb Sunday trading and to prevent the public from visiting taverns, parks, museums, zoos, theatres, meeting houses and concert halls, presumably in the hope that people would have no alternative but to attend the Anglican Church.

This legislation cast a blight on British Sundays for nearly 200 years. As the political factors eased, the government might have reduced restrictions, but a religious revival in the nineteenth century raised objections. The Lord's Day Observance Society was founded in 1831. It was a highly influential pressure group, but over the years it has only managed to delay the slow erosion of the provisions of the 1780 Act. Campaigns against zoos being open on Sunday and people taking trips on the Thames were among its first efforts. In the 1930s it tried to keep cinemas closed; in the 1950s to prevent advertisements on television and ban Sunday cricket matches; and today, under the name Day One Christian Ministries, it still campaigns for Sunday to be a day of worship and rest.

Some sections of the 1780 Act prohibiting the use of any building or room for public entertainment or debate on a Sunday remained in force until after the 1960s. The Sunday Trading Act 1994 still limits how long shops may remain open and what they may sell. Theatres open only rarely on Sunday. Today, Sunday is still exceptional, but it is the welfare of workers and their rights which influence secular campaigners.

97. There Is Less Guilt in the World Now

The aim of all religions is to instil guilt in their followers: they must try harder to please whichever deity they worship, and they can never be good enough. Both Catholics and Protestants believe that their sins may threaten their existence or their treatment in the next world. The Christian tenet of Original Sin, the inheritance passed down through the millennia from Adam and Eve in the Garden of Eden, is particularly claimed by Catholics. They think they are born guilty, and that what they are is wrong. Those of the Calvinist persuasion in particular also believe that mankind is inherently wicked. The religious upbringing of both Catholics and extreme Protestants has primed them to regard the majority of their actions and emotions as inherently wrong. Both Protestants and Catholics believe that many actions can be sinful and having a good time is often an affront, especially to the Puritan deity.

Much Protestant theology comes from the Old Testament. Like the Jews, their guilt comes from the feeling they have not done enough. Protestants earn guilt not just by what they do, but also by failing to do their duty, which adds an extra dimension to Protestant guilt.

In Catholicism the rite of confession, in which supposed sins are revealed to a priest who can then impose a penance, remains intact. Gone are the glory days of public shame, walking barefoot through the streets carrying a placard detailing the sin. Today it's more likely to be some quiet private act of atonement. A ceremony, whether public or private, does provide a sense of closure, of being able to start again. Some

Protestant churches require public acknowledgement of sin before a congregation, but there is no standard rite of penance: it is for the sinner to make reparation. In any case, no one can be absolutely certain how God regards a transgression. Guilt becomes superglued to the Protestant soul for a lifetime.

Catholicism has the constant presence of saints – the model held up for everyone to follow, but a standard a negligible number of people are ever going to attain. Moderate Protestantism encourages people to do their best. There is a recognition that the perfection Catholicism demands is not realistic. Even this moderation, however, leads to a permanent feeling of unease and constant self-questioning about whether this is the best that can be achieved, if there is more that should be done. There isn't a moment's peace from this inner nag, like living with a stereotypical mother-in-law implying you haven't done something or aren't as successful as someone else.

Current research is inconclusive, but seems to suggest that there is no great difference here between the followers of the three Judeo-Christian religions: Jews, Catholics and Protestants all feel guilt and the more religious you are the more guilt you feel. So the Reformation neither increased not decreased the amount of guilt felt on religious grounds in the world, it merely produced different reasons to feel guilty.

98. PROTESTANTISM CHANGED THE CONCEPT OF TIME

For Roman Catholics all events, past, present and future, co-exist in God, who is outside time. In Holy Communion the bread and wine become the actual flesh and blood of Christ because his sacrifice is always in the present, always happening. Armageddon, the end of the world, is both in the future and has already happened. Time in Catholicism is both linear and non-linear.

Protestantism, however, says that the Last Supper and the Crucifixion were one-off events. They happened once and time moved on: it is purely linear. Communion is a remembrance of Christ's sacrifice. This has profound implications, because if the future is not fixed it can be changed and, as mainstream Protestants believe, should be made better to bring it closer to God's supposed ideal. Progress means discoveries and inventions to improve life. Even if they are only described as new and improved, they are different.

Another legacy of this concept of time is that countries with a Protestant heritage, like Britain, Germany, Scandinavia and North America, where activities are run to a strict timetable, experience problems dealing with countries with a Roman Catholic heritage, where a timetable is regarded as something to aim for but not immutable. If the future has already happened, why try to constrain it – it will unfold at God's pace and in accord with his intentions. If something more interesting comes up that may be part of his plan, and a person of Mediterranean inheritance will pursue it while the northern people are looking at their watches and tutting.

99. The World Would Be a Different Place if the Reformation Had Failed

This is incontrovertible, but how would it be different is another matter. Arguments can be pursued on a number of websites, but relatively few scholarly works have looked at this question in depth. Those who have agree that if Martin Luther had not made such a dramatic impact, or indeed not have existed, then someone else would have become the figurehead for reform. All corrupt regimes eventually fail, so the outcome would have been the same. But how that would have panned out depends on a number of other factors. Had Henry VIII and Catherine of Aragon produced a male heir – and ideally a spare – who survived to inherit the throne of England, things would have been different whether Luther existed or not. The same factors would apply in all the other Christian countries. Had Henri IV not been assassinated in France in 1610, history might have happened differently. The quantum butterfly of chance is usually not a single insect – whole flocks of them are needed to blow the course of events along a different path.

Literature is less constrained. There are three major works which explore what might have happened had the Reformation failed. The first is *Pavane* by Keith Roberts (1968), a series of stories set in a world where Roman Catholicism is re-established in England following the assassination of Elizabeth I in 1588 and the Spanish Armada's victory. A feudal system is still in place, but rebellion is in the air. The stories are not, as this brief summary suggests, a complete condemnation of Catholicism. The next is *The Alteration* by Kingsley Amis, published in 1976, inspired by a recording of

Alessandro Moreschi, the last Italian castrato, who sang in the Sistine Chapel Choir and who died in 1923. The hero is a teenage boy facing castration to preserve his pre-pubescent voice. In Amis's world, Martin Luther saw the error of his ways, accepted Catholicism and became Pope. Religious dissenters have established themselves in the Republic of New England. Politically nothing has changed since the sixteenth century and the Cold War of the time is between Christianity and Islam. The most recent work is the *His Dark Materials* trilogy by Philip Pullman, published between 1995 and 2000. Lyra's world is a parallel universe ruled by a body called the Magisterium, which is the name of the actual Roman Catholic authority which determines the Church's teachings. Here Jean Calvin is the Pope, based in Geneva. The trilogy culminates in the death of the Authority, a false god. It's a lot more theologically and narratively complicated than this, and Pullman has said his novels are not anti-religion but are against the misuse of power.

In all three authors' alternative worlds the industrial revolution never happened, so technology is not advanced. Science is heavily distrusted by their totalitarian religious regimes, especially electricity, so there are no television or radio sets, no telephones and no computers. Societies are essentially feudal and women have an inferior position (so no change there then).

100. BIBLICAL TRANSLATION IS A JOB FOR LIFE

By the time of the Reformation a version of the Bible in Latin, known as the Vulgate, was used in the Roman Catholic Church. For centuries, however, parts had been translated from the original Hebrew (Old Testament) and Greek (New) into local languages, but these were discouraged by the Church authorities, not least because of the possible interpretations they threw up. The main problem remains that translation is not an exact science; grammatical conventions make word-by-word transliteration impossible because they affect meaning. All languages have words which cannot be easily rendered into another, not least because the cultural concepts are different. The Bible was written in different times, places and social and political situations from those in Europe from the Middle Ages onwards.

Renaissance scholars discovered there was no Biblical justification for much of the Roman Catholic Church's beliefs and practices, which initiated the Reformation and founded the important field of Bible Studies. The first almost complete Biblical translation by William Tyndale into English appeared in 1535, and criticisms of its scholarship came immediately after. It was followed by the Great Bible (1539), the first to be authorised, but which was displaced in popularity by the Geneva Bible (1560). This was extremely significant, especially for Calvinists, but there was also the Bishops' Bible (1568). These all took Tyndale's work as their starting point. From 1582 Roman Catholics could use the Douay-Rheims translation of the New Testament, also influenced by Tyndale's version. Elizabeth I attempted to impose the Bishops'

Bible, but it was the Authorised Version produced under James I in 1611 that triumphed. Initially it was resisted: people preferred what they were used to and the older versions remained in use, but as worshippers became accustomed to this new edition they grew to love it – to hear its cadences. This didn't stop scholars criticising it.

A revised version was produced in 1885, but the first important retranslation was the *Revised Standard Version* in 1952. This was updated in the *New Revised Standard Version* in 1989, which was expanded to become the ecumenical edition which could be used by both Protestants and Roman Catholics. All translations carry the imprint of their times. This version was criticised for sounding like a business management handbook and for removing gender bias in line with the intellectual fashions of the day.

Modern versions are able to use early texts, some of which, like the Dead Sea Scrolls, are only recently discovered. It now seems impossible that there will never be one agreed version of the Bible, even in its original languages, let alone in translations. Today over 450 English versions are available, produced for all shades of religious belief. Some have the text adjusted to fit with a particular tenet, like the *Purified Translation* of the New Testament for Christian teetotallers, which shows Christ and his disciples drinking grape juice, not wine.

Those looking for a job for life might look to Biblical translation, which has been a never-ending task for centuries since the Reformation.